The Tangled Braid

D1166156

for Daniel,
enjoy!
Isaac

The Tangled Braid
Ninety-nine Poems by Hafiz of Shiraz

A New Translation
by Jeffrey Einboden and John Slater

[signature]

FONS VITAE

First published in 2009 by
Fons Vitae
49 Mockingbird Valley Drive
Louisville, KY 40207
http://www.fonsvitae.com
Email: fonsvitaeky@aol.com

Copyright Fons Vitae 2009

Library of Congress Control Number: 2009933714

ISBN 9781891785429

No part of this book may be reproduced
in any form without prior permission of
the publishers. All rights reserved.

Printed in Canada

*for Hillary Einboden
and Melissa Braaten*

Hafiz,

Let the world go under
and you and I compete alone
loss and yearning shared
between us like twins
and my only boast: that I'm
like you in love and drunkenness.

Let my poem burn according to its fire—
you are older and ever-new.

                              —Goethe

Contents

I

Contents, continued

II

Contents, continued

III

Acknowledgments

The translators would like to thank the following people for their guidance and encouragement: Tamara Follini, Keith Gandal, Douglas Hedley, Ryan Hibbett, Jeffrey Johnson, William C. Johnson, Gordon Johnston, Jessica Reyman, James Vigus, as well as Gray Henry and the anonymous readers at *Fons Vitae.*

We would also like to thank the Graduate School and English faculty at Northern Illinois University for their support during the preparation of *The Tangled Braid.*

Thanks finally to the following journals in whose pages selected poems from *The Tangled Braid* first appeared: *PN Review, CrossCurrents, The Dalhousie Review, Words without Borders, Able Muse,* and *SUFI.*

Introduction

Jeffrey Einboden

Writing in his journal in 1847, Ralph Waldo Emerson affirmed that a "good scholar" – in reading Hafiz – would discover this Persian poet to be "full of American history". Just a year before penning this curious remark, Emerson had himself enjoyed his first encounter with Hafiz. Purchasing a German rendition of Hafiz' *Divan* in the spring of 1846, the celebrated American essayist dedicated the following months to translating generous portions from this edition into English. Later that same year, when Emerson's own initial volume of poetry appeared in Boston, readers discovered this seminal collection to include not only several poems clearly indebted to Hafiz, but also hundreds of lines translated directly from his *Divan*.

Although it may seem surprising to find a 14th-century Persian poet standing at the very inception of a distinctly American tradition of verse, Emerson's early engagement with Hafiz provides an intriguing historical precedent for the current interest in Persian poetry now so prevalent in the West. Modern translations of Sufi poets have won substantial audiences in the U.K. and North America, granting many English readers their first access to this rich heritage of Islamic spirituality. While deriving from a culture and history seemingly remote from contemporary Western audiences, renditions of Persian poetry have proved remarkably popular, appearing as both timely and relevant contributions to 21st-century English poetics and inter-religious dialogue.

The present translation of Hafiz itself arose from distinctly Emersonian origins. It was in reading the American's rapturous praise for Hafiz that I was initially prompted to study Persian, completing a doctorate at the University of Cambridge concerning Emerson's renditions of Hafiz in 2005. The idea of producing fresh renditions from the *Divan* was first suggested two years later, proposed by my cousin and co-translator, John Slater, during a visit to his home at the Abbey of the Genesee in upstate New York. The rendition process we subsequently developed recalls, in some respects, Emerson's own method of "double" translation, his rendering of Hafiz by means of an intermediary translation. The present volume resulted from a comparable, two-staged procedure: I would first generate literal English translations and annotated paraphrases of Hafiz' Persian; John would then take these plain sources and notes, working with them to produce exquisite, English poems.

Although evoking an American tradition of Hafiz rendition which reaches back to U.S. literary beginnings in the 19th century, *The Tangled*

The Tangled Braid

Braid also reflects its 21st-century production, being entirely composed through email exchange over a two-year period. Except for a final face-to-face session held at the Abbey of the Genesee in May 2009, John and I worked by means of electronic correspondence, weaving the *Braid* together via internet connections and cables. And despite the seeming incongruity between modern technology and medieval source, our virtual collaboration nevertheless came to harmonize and resonate with the content and conceits of Hafiz' own poetry. Integral to the *Divan* are a diverse range of lyric relationships, invocations and encounters. The poet perpetually calls out to the "other" – addressing his God, his patrons, his enemies, his readers, even his own self – dramatizing a vast array of associations which exhibit the vast array of human potentialities. Interlocking dialogues and dichotomies unfold within each poem, pairing together rose & nightingale; lover & beloved; orthodox & unorthodox; here & hereafter; human & divine. Conversation, interaction and exchange are consequently essential to the *Divan*'s own verses, exemplified through its recurrent reference to "messengers" and to "wine" – the vehicles of both *communication* and *communion*. Translating Hafiz by means of a remote dialogue, and exchanging his poems through the intangible ether, seemed a fitting medium for deciphering verses so urgently concerned with both companionship and separation, with both presence and absence – indeed, a fitting medium for translating a poet who has earned the mystic titles of "Tongue of the Unseen" (*"lisān al-ghaib"*) and "Translator of Secrets" (*"turjumān al-asrār"*).

Born in Shiraz, a cultural capital of medieval Persia, around the year 1326, Hafiz was himself engaged in conversation with a long line of poetic predecessors, inheriting and responding to an already bountiful tradition of Sufi verse. As a result, his *Divan* may be thought not only as comprising a variety of poetic dialogues, but also as representing a complex dialogue with the poetic past, recalling and invoking prominent precursors such as Nizami, 'Attar, 'Iraqi, Sa'di. The spiritual potency and lyric beauty of the *Divan* has ensured, however, that this conversation with history stretches not only backward to Persian antiquity, but also forward to an international modernity. Hafiz' poetry continues to enjoy a vibrant afterlife, spanning cultures, geographies, religions and languages, becoming not only "full of American history", but also an essential chapter within an emergent World Literature. The present translation strives to keep faith with both the *Divan*'s cultural past and its global future, balancing between medieval Persian content and modern English poetics. Although at times prompted to reshape the specifics of Hafiz' references and tropes – as identified frequently in the volume's appended Notes –

The Tangled Braid also seeks to reproduce the delicate texture of sacred meaning and sensual image which is vital to his poetry, knitting together the spiritual and artistic commitments underlying Hafiz' original. It is my hope that the present volume – generated through conversation, and interweaving divergent strands of culture and expression – may contribute to the *Divan*'s evolving currency, providing contemporary readers with an authentic means of approaching, and encountering, Hafiz.

Introduction

John Slater

As a teenager I read an anthology of sacred poetry that truly changed my life: It was as though a third dimension, a transparency had opened in a painting previously flat and opaque. I was given a drink of the spiritual wine that would nourish both my love for poetry and desire to live as a monk. This anthology was my initial exposure to Sufi poetry. It was significant I think that I encountered it alongside Zen and Christian mystical works. Sufism shared both the ardent erotic language of Christian love mysticism and the concentration and detachment one associates with Zen. Of course, the advantage of an anthology of this kind is that one can see the overlap and interplay between traditions. I remember reading the story, in this book, of the Chinese Zen poet Li Po, who, drunk one night out on the lake in his rowboat, was so enraptured by the reflection of the moon on the water that he lunged forward to embrace it, fell into the water and drowned! The first poem I would publish, many years later, was a spinoff from this legend.

Hafiz tends to provocatively blur the border between material and spiritual wine and love. At seventeen, I was far more enamored of the former. But nine years later, in the novitiate of a Cistercian monastery, when my novice master picked up and passed along Ladinsky's versions of Hafiz, 'The Gift,' I was able, having drunk more deeply of the spiritual wine, to appreciate the language of excess and intoxication, 'from the other side' so to speak. Now, Hafiz, with his playful subversion of the uptight orthodox accuser (the one we all carry in our heads) helped me stay true to the experience that had first drawn me to the monastic life, to keep resetting the pitch of my spiritual life 'in the key of love'.

Five years later (the five most intense and transformative in my life), I encountered the work of the Iranian calligrapher Jila Peacock; her exquisite 'concrete' renderings of the poems (the Persian characters of each ghazal shaped into the image of an animal mentioned within it: a horse or nightingale or peacock) were not only breathtaking visually but, as translated by her into English, the finest versions of Hafiz I'd seen, the first and only ones in fact I found very interesting *as poetry*. The ten poems had a density and texture, a richness of expression that, given the way Hafiz had popped up at earlier key moments in my life, made me wonder more and more what the original Persian poems were like. When I learned that my cousin, Jeffrey Einboden, was doing doctoral work on Hafiz, I began to pester him about it.

Jeff and I grew up in Ontario (Canada) a couple of hours apart and saw each other mainly at Christmas and on summer holidays. Often we'd drift off from family gatherings to play chess or talk philosophy. When I left for the monastery, we remained friends. Although, or perhaps because, he was studying the problematic western reception of eastern poetry, he wasn't very forthcoming when I asked about the various English versions, and what Hafiz was like in the original. But when, on a summer visit at the abbey, I suggested we attempt our own translations, he was eager to give it a try. It was obscure and difficult material but there were enough fascinating and alluring lines coming through that we determined to stay with it. In no time, the work took on a life of its own. We felt clearly that, from behind the veil, Hafiz was cheering us on.

Reading other translations of Hafiz into English, I found them either so 'loose' one distrusted their fidelity to the original or so dry and 'scholarly' they were lifeless. In an essay by A.J. Arberry where he provides a literal prose rendering of a Hafiz ghazal followed by its mutation into rhyming quatrains, I noticed how enticing the first, raw, stage was; really, more attractive to me as poetry than the polished verses. Jeff and I wanted to convey the strangeness and surprise of the original in attractive and resonant contemporary English poems.

Working in two stages, with two people, had definite advantages. Jeff could concentrate all his efforts on providing accurate, literal translations, glossing the text, and researching commentaries on the more obscure verses. His careful selection of which poems might be fruitful to work on was also essential. For my part, I could focus on teasing out poems from sometimes daunting material. What to do with:

> O Heart, youth fled…and you have plucked up not single rose
> from the life-of-pleasure,
> In your agedness of head, make some skill in renown and name.

or:

> I shall depart into the street of the Magi, [with my] garment
> sleeve scattering,
> From these tribulations which the hem of the latter-times took.

Needless to say, with such passages, I was grateful for each morsel of explanation and commentary Jeff could provide.

I determined early on to trade a wooden adherence to formal features of the ghazal in Persian for both greater adherence to the sense of the original and a more pleasing English line. Many ghazals have a first stanza with each of its two lines ending in the same word or phrase. This word ends the second line of subsequent stanzas. For translation into English, in addition to making for impossibly awkward sentences, retaining the keyword in the end position is overkill. To ears accustomed to free verse, the repetition of the same word (or a similar word or idea) *anywhere* in every other line is a lot, and provokes, one could argue, an effect roughly proportionate to that enjoyed by Hafiz' first readers. Emerson famously spoke of the 'meter-making argument,' the idea that form grows out of what a poem has to say. As I began to brainstorm and free-write a slew of possible reformulations of the strange literal renderings I was given, internal rhymes, patterns of assonance and consonance, began to emerge of themselves, and echo in music the indirect play of meanings between the stanzas.

'Indirect', since in most ghazals, the relation of one stanza to the next is not apparent. To some degree, they are meant to stand alone, as essentially complete units, miniature poems. There is a disjunctive shock as the mind plays down the lines. Seemingly disconnected images pile up and, on repeated readings, subtly inter-resonate. They *are* related though the order in which they appear is more important in some poems than others. This high degree of indirection offsets another feature of the ghazal which some believe to be problematic for western readers, namely, their ardor and corresponding hyperbole. Part of the difficulty may be that many of the more 'scholarly' translations are almost completely *devoid* of passion, never mind capturing a trace of the fierce desire expressed in the original. Some feel that even if it were well rendered, the over the top declarations of erotic need, the extravagant descriptions of the beloved's beauty reducing the world to ash and so on would not sit well with readers habituated to a high degree of irony and understatement. I suspect, however, that, precisely because we're used to such a muting of emotion, reading Hafiz can be a liberation: he allows us to step into his shoes, and say things we need to and could not have otherwise. Of course, the west is not altogether without 'passionate' poets (Whitman, for one, springs to mind). Further, I think there's a comic side to many of the extreme expressions of love and admiration that is a definite element in the charm of Hafiz' persona:

> Hafiz, from the fortune of your love, has become like Solomon,
> a bankrupt millionaire, with nothing in his hands but wind.

We're amused to find Hafiz once again so bowled over and hilarious with need and yearning.

Many of the tropes and images that at first seemed simply alien or awkward to me, in time, began to charm. Hafiz imagines the curve of the beloved's eyebrow as a bow, and the glance shot from her eye, an arrow to pierce his heart. Often he compares the perfect curve of her eyebrow to the curved niche indicating direction of prayer in a mosque. I went from thinking, 'Oh no, he's obsessing about the eyebrow *again*?!' to a kind of delight in the strangeness and delicacy of the image. Like the disjunction between stanzas in a ghazal, cultural and aesthetic dissonance can carry a hidden charge. Besides, if one is not prepared to find beauty in new and strange expressions, why read poetry from other times and places at all?

One of the most attractive features of the poems is surely the persona of 'Hafiz' himself: his candor and familiarity, his compassionate wisdom and humor, the ardor of his desire, and his playful subversion of the rigidly 'orthodox'. This strong persona that (again like Whitman) invites readers into the world of the poem, combines with another, disorienting element of the poems, in an interesting way: frequently it's unclear who is speaking. Whether it is a 'he', 'she' or 'it', whether a divine or human person, is intriguingly uncertain in the original and this is something Hafiz exploits to the full. Translating, I've opted against consistency: 'she' can mean human or divine beloved, and likewise with 'he.' Similarly, the language of 'wine' and desire may or may not be a metaphor of spiritual realities. In Rumi, it is clearer that a spiritual meaning is intended. As mentioned, Hafiz delights in leaving the matter obscure. Perhaps at times it's 'both/and,' love, human and divine at once, real wine and spiritual intoxication...

In Ghazal 467, which we've translated 'The Courier,' Hafiz begins by invoking 'the breeze of the new day'. The personification of inanimate objects was another Persian trope I found initially disconcerting but, at least in some instances, came to love; in the course of a collection of ghazals it's interesting to see the character of a figure like the 'dawn wind' emerge. In this poem, one in which the stanzas are more clearly connected than in others, Hafiz invites the breeze to bring a message to his beloved. The lines seethe with the eager restless desire of a lover awaiting a response. The breeze is entrusted with the task of conveying the most intimate secrets of the speaker's heart, at his own discretion, according to his own sense of what's best. The repeated phrase underlines the point; Hafiz begs the wind to intercede 'in the way you know'. I like to imagine this as a kind of metaphorical invitation to the translator. Hafiz, eager to allure and delight the reader, respects the need for his interpreter, the 'courier' of his desire, to work to some degree in his own style, in the way he best knows. This of course may be no more than playful eisegesis, but the last verse is suggestive:

> In this exchange, Turkish, Arabic—it makes no difference:
>> speak the word of love in the language you know.

At a time when Islam and 'the West' are so polarized and the temptation to a kind of mutual demonization so strong, we need to hear the voice of Hafiz, the singular hope and generosity that shines in his poems. Art has a way of 'cutting corners,' of short-circuiting the tortuous path of cross-cultural exchange. Not, surely, to replace it—but once one has been struck by the beauty of a work from another cultural world, has known a basic and spontaneous moment of aesthetic/spiritual empathy spanning differences of time, culture and religion—not carelessly reducing the other to one's own terms, but attracted by the very mix of recognition and strangeness in the encounter—he cannot in good faith dismiss that world with angry generalizations.

Hafiz himself demonstrates a remarkably 'ecumenical' spirit. I was surprised and delighted to find, in one poem, a reference to Christian monasticism. It's true, the monastery serves as an image of external worship, in contrast with the 'tavern' where the spiritual wine of mystical experience is enjoyed; and that Christian monasteries were popular with Sufis as hospitable places where wine, forbidden in the surrounding culture, flowed freely; still, there is the sense, here, as elsewhere, that the outward observance is, or can be, pervaded by a spiritual light. For a Muslim poet to perceive glory shining 'in the word of the Cross' that guides the lives of the monks is truly striking.

> Monastery, tavern…in love, it makes no difference:
>> the radiant face of the Friend shines everywhere on earth.

> The monks at their work show forth glory
>> in the word of the Cross, their rule of life.

> Hafiz bears witness: in the end, everything is not in vain—
>> a fabulous myth and an amazing word.

The Tangled Braid

Detail from Sultan Muhammad. Heavenly and Earthly Drunkenness (painting, recto), folio from a Divan of Hafiz, c. 1526-1527. Ink, color, gold and silver on paper; actual: 28.7 x 35.5 cm (11-5/16 x 14 in.). Harvard Art Museum, Arthur M. Sackler Museum, Promised Gift of Mr. and Mrs. Stuart Cary Welch, Jr. Partially owned by the Metropolitan Museum of Art and the Arthur M.Sackler Museum, Harvard University, 1988. In honor of the students of Harvard University and Radcliffe College, 1988.460.3. Photo: Allan Macintyre C. President and Fellows of Harvard College

Escape-Route

Scattering petals, swishing red wine in the ample cup—
through the torn rooftop of the universe we launch a new way.

Should anguish form a death-squad to wipe out lovers
all of us at the wine-house would rebel, and yank the chair out from under them.

We sloshed rose-water into the wine-cup
packed sugar in the censer of the fragrant wind...

When the sweet lute is at hand, poet, play sweetly
so that waving our hands we may shout a ghazal, and dancing we may toss our heads.

O wind, blow the dust of our lives into the courtyard of the Beautiful
that standing among his fair ones we may gaze upon the King.

One brags about his intellect, another of his grace and charm—
but what are these before the sovereign Judge?

If you want to get back to Eden, come with us to the wine-house.
In time, we shall draw you up: from the dregs of the cup to the clear pool of Paradise.

These days in Shiraz, word-craft and melodious speech are not in fashion.
Hafiz, let's make our escape, and cast ourselves into another realm.

The Dregs

Wild-eyed sweaty hair messed, with a drunken smile
shirt torn shouting a ghazal she raised the cup.

The flower of her glance was bold taunting petulant
she came and sat next to my bed at midnight.

Leaning over the bed she put her lips to my ear and whispered:
Old lover, are you still asleep?

They poured nightlong wine for the would-be mystic.
If he rejects the gift he's an infidel to love itself.

Get lost you teetotalling wretch, stop pestering those who drink
the dregs. Wine is our only heritage from the Day of Alast.

What he splashed into our cup we drank:
the wine of love or water from the heavenly fountain.

The delight of wine, the tangled hair of the beloved…
how many vows they've shattered, those of Hafiz too!

The Courier

Breeze of the new spring day, when the time is ripe, in the way
you alone best know—slip onto the street of You-Know-Who.

Secret courier, I watch for your return, restless, vigilant…
Be gracious: forthright, not overbearing, in the way you know.

Say: all strength has slipped from my hand—for God's sake
from that soul-nourishing jewel, pass along what you know.

I've written these delicate words so that no one else may know,
read them aloud with love in your own irreplaceable way.

I crave the sleek dagger of your body like a thirsty man water—
slay your glad captive in whatever way you like.

How could I not lash all my hope to your gilded, woven belt?
The meaning's not so obvious, as you, my love, will know.

In this exchange, Turkish, Arabic—it makes no difference:
speak the word of love in the language you know.

Bankrupt

If you want me safe, upright and responsible, you're out of luck—
I've been drunk on the purest wine from the Day of Alast.

The moment I was first washed clean in Love's cold fountain
I pronounced four blessings, on all, for everyone.

Give me wine, and I will tell you more than your fortune.
Her face has made me a lover and her fragrance made me drunk.

O reveler, beyond, where the span of a mountain's the width of an ant,
do not stop knocking on the door of grace.

He is seen in the rapt gaze of your own reflection—or not at all.
Otherwise, under the pale blue dome, no one can be happy.

Let my soul be the ransom of your mouth, for in the ground of my gaze
the Gardener has planted no rose-bud so beautiful.

Hafiz, from the fortune of your love, has become like Solomon,
a bankrupt millionaire, with nothing in his hands but wind.

Worthless

Without your face, the most exquisite rose is worthless—
without that wine, even spring turns sour.

Though circling the late spring orchard or strolling the daybreak garden,
outside the light of your face, there's no solace.

The rose lost in contemplation, the wind-swept cypress dancing—
without your voice, they are empty ghosts.

Together with you—everything you say, the way you stand—
that I can't hold you, that I can't kiss you, even once—ruthless.

Keep your rose-garden and sweet liqueur—
there's no comfort without the Friend.

Lovely faces in the masterworks, painting, sculpture—
but yours is the only one I look for.

Hafiz, the heart is small change, a coin, a nickel
tossed into the crowd at a wedding.

The Box of Jewels

When I follow in his steps he provokes tribulation,
if I rest on the path he explodes in a rage.

If I stop at the crossroads to catch my breath
and fall on his feet like dust…he vanishes like wind.

When I seek the least kiss—he spews out grief
like sugar from the jewelry-box of his mouth.

That seductive leer in your haughty eye
would mingle my tears with the dust of the road.

Both the sand dunes and valleys of love prove treacherous.
One needs the heart of a lion, unafraid of pain.

Beg for life and patience. The world is a mischievous juggler
and the tricks he's played on you so far are only his opening act.

Hafiz, lay your head upon the doorstep of surrender
for if you fight against the world it will only fight you back.

Accounting

Stabbing my heart with your glance like a sharpened arrow-tip—
Stop it! That piercing look might kill me.

You've broken the bank with the vast wealth of your beauty.
Pour out the surplus on me, a destitute beggar.

Fill up my cup of wine, for I remain a fresh youth
in the realm of love, though in this world a weak old man.

Occupied by the Friend, the vast expanding empire of my chest
lost all thought of its own independence.

If the manager's pen must render an account
let the bankbook show as my one expense: wine and song.

In this hectic world, where no one cares for another
the Master has supplied me with boundless wealth.

Pious fraud, how long will you swindle us like children?
banning the fruit of the tree, milk and honey.

I've made a deal with the merchants:
on the day of grief I'll drink nothing but wine.

At dawn, at dusk, from my perch on
the celestial throne: ecstatic song.

My treasure buried deep in the heart like Hafiz
who cares if the judge says I'm crude?

How good it was, when the abundance of wine
gave me freedom from the king and his minister.

Stairway to the Sun

We heard last night from his messenger:
the King has called us to his inmost court.

The dust of our flesh, mingled with the purest wine,
the time came to build for the heart its lonely home.

Countless holy books extolling the beauty of the Friend—
and these no more than a letter in the alphabet.

O wine-stained sufi-robe, cover my faults!
The one in the unstained garment could be here any time.

We learned tonight where each of us stood: gathered
at prayer, in a circle, the Moon shone in our midst.

Behold: the boldness of the tiny ant who climbs the throne
of one whose crown forms the very stairway of the sun.

My heart, guard your faith from his seductive glance.
Sly, enchanting, bent on plunder he draws the bow.

Covered with stains, seek the favor of the King, like Hafiz;
for his generous gift is meant to make us clean.

Those in the circle: an ocean. Know the time of knowing.
Hey! you with the broken heart—it's time to get down to business.

Five Days of Freedom

The heart: a lush curtained palace of his love—
the eye: a clear mirror that reflects his image.

I don't bow my head for anyone in this world or the next—
but I bend my neck beneath the load of his gifts.

For you: the tree of Paradise, for us: the slender body of the Friend.
What we see depends on the depth of our longing.

So what if my robe is stained?
Everything reveals his purity.

I stood in the inmost court when the dawn breeze
blew aside the curtain…to the Holy of Holies.

The days of that crazy Lover have passed—now it's our turn!
everyone gets at least five days to be madly in love with the Friend.

The wealth of delight, the vast empire of loving him…
all that I have is the gift of his bounty.

Never mind the outward poverty of Hafiz—
his heart is the royal treasure-house of love for the Friend.

Secrets of the Empty Cell

Joined with subtle elegance, your beauty stole the world.
When they work together, who can resist?

The candle would have shown the secrets of our empty cell
but, thanks be to God, the secret could not be spoken.

Lit from the secret fire raging in my chest
the sun's a mere torch raised up by the heavens.

The rose wanted to spread the perfume of the Friend
but the jealous dawn wind swallowed its fragrant breath.

At first, calm, circling the edge like a compass
I've been sucked up into the center, caught in the vortex.

Love for the cup of wine scorched my harvest
when the shining face of the Beautiful blazed on the rim.

Leaving for the street of the wise, I wave the sleeves of my robe
escaping the sorrows tucked in the hem of Time's garment.

Drink up! everyone who's caught a glimpse of the End
sets out light and joyful for a night of heavy drinking.

It is written on the rose-leaf, in the blood-red streak of the tulip:
The one who's grown wise to the world drinks the deepest crimson wine.

Grab your chance! when grief struck the world
the sufi took up his wine-cup and sorrow took up the lute.

Hafiz, your words sweat the water of life…
how can the envious quibble?

Bound

When God formed the heart-opening arc of your eyebrow
he bound me rapt by your seductive glance.

Like the restless bird of the orchard, all peace was stolen from my heart
when he wove the flowers of your gorgeous robe.

When the breeze-blown fragrance of the rose chased after you along the path
of yearning, it loosened the knots of our hearts from every other flower.

With the passing of time, I've grown content to be your slave—
why not? my thread was meant to be woven by your least desire.

Don't tie my beggar's heart like the string on a pouch of incense—
already I'm bound to your braid which loosens every knot.

Our time together was paradise, and my foolish heart
bound to hope that somehow it wouldn't pass.

Cruel hand, holding back...I've had enough—I'm leaving!
but he only laughed: Go ahead, Hafiz, what's stopping you?

Overnight Delivery

Like an urgent courier, a breeze blown in from the east brought word:
The long day of toil and affliction has drawn at last to a close.

For the good news carried on the breeze at dawn
we tipped the messengers, gave the torn robe to the daybreak heralds.

With the Friend watching over us, we endure the long pilgrimage back to Shiraz.
Blessed destiny! to share the way home with so grand a traveler.

Come! Come! because the doorman of paradise has drawn you
into this world as the poor heart's fellow traveler.

Work full force, with all the strength of your inmost mind—
for this worn cloth cap keeps poking through the glorious crown.

At the least thought of her radiant face—sighs and groans stretching
from my poor parched heart… to the luminous tent of the moon.

Hafiz raised high the flag of the Victor
safe in the refuge of the king of kings.

The King's Highway

If you want to peer into the wine-cup of the King
paint your eyes with dust off the tavern floor.

Never drift far from poetry or wine. Beneath the arch of heaven
these alone banish grief from the heart.

The rose you long for will remove its veil
only when you serve it, like the morning wind.

Set out on the daylong journey of love. At the very first step
on the path, you'll begin to reap a profit.

Come, get the drug of his presence, and the plan of his law
from the overflowing bounty of those who know.

Wash the dust of the road from your eyes
there's no veil covering the face of the Friend.

Since you never leave the dwelling of your inmost self,
how is it you've crossed our path?

Just to beg at the door of the tavern's a rare, transforming drink—
if you can do it, the dust where you sit will be turned to gold.

In all your pious diligence, begin to see the light
and you might lose your head like a flickering candle.

If you long for the kiss, and the cup, of the beloved
don't expect to have time for anything less.

Hafiz, pay heed to this supreme advice
and you'll take the royal way of the Truly Real.

Caravans

Noble crowned bird of the wind, I will send you to the Queen of Sheba—
be sure to know where I'm sending you: from this world to the next.

How sad, that a bird like you should be trapped in this heap of dust,
I will send you from here to your original home.

On the way of love there is no close or distant—
I see you there before me and send my prayer.

At dawn, at dusk, on the north wind and the wind from the east
I send out caravans of prayer that you prosper.

So long as the army of grief has not overthrown your heart
I will pay off the enemy, giving my own heart in ransom.

Come, bringer of wine, for the Invisible has brought good news:
Suffer grief with patience and I will send you peace.

O hidden from sight but remaining close to your lovers
I offer up my prayer, sending you my song of praise.

See God's creative love in your own true face—
I will send you a shining mirror radiant with his light.

I'm sending you these songs and poems
so the troubadours around your throne may tell you my desire.

Hafiz, in our circle, we remember your name with hymns…
Hurry! I'll send a swift horse and a decent shirt.

The Compass

The ignorant were bewildered by the looks flashed between us—
I am what I am, they can think what they like.

Surely the wise form the still-point of the turning Compass
but Love knows its circling will still make their heads spin.

The promise of God was sealed by the lips of the eloquent.
We are their servants, and they, like gods to us.

Helpless beggars, all we crave for is wine and song—
if only the tavern would take my robe in exchange!

Boasting of love, lamenting their apartness from the Friend...what fakes
they are; such hypocrites deserve their separation.

The bridal chamber of his face lies reflected not only in my gaze
but the Sun and Moon too circulate a mirror.

Words about the sun at night can never reach the sightless bird.
In this mirror, even those who see are overwhelmed.

Unless your black gleaming eye should teach us the work
no one could reach true sober intoxication.

If the young seekers knew the secret of our thoughts
they wouldn't take our worn-out robe in its place.

Should the wind bear your scent to the celestial paradise
it would shower down jewels like scattered coins.

If the saint can't understand poor drunken Hafiz, so what?
The devil flees from those who memorize the scripture.

A Night of Candles

All day long, drunk on her fragrant hair—
with every breath, her seductive wink leaves me wasted.

O Lord, after the long night of grief, let us see
a night of candles in the curved alcove of your eyebrow.

The image of your face written into my retinas...
precious! my only book from the library of the Beautiful.

If you want the world made eternally beautiful at once
ask the wind to blow aside the veil of the beloved.

To cast out the fawning prayers of the hypocrites
wave your head like a dancer and shake them from your hair.

The dawn breeze and I are both worthless beggars
enchanted by your glance, drunk on your fragrance.

The world has filled Hafiz with yearning for the end of time—
he sees nothing but the dust at the gate to your street.

The Jeweler

Call to mind: how you gazed upon us from deep within,
the image of your burning sun reflected in our face.

Recall: when your glance cut us down with stern rebuke—
like sugar on the lips, the free gift of Jesus.

Remember: raising high the glass at table with friends,
there was no one but you and I…and God, with us.

Your face made the flickering candle blaze higher,
my scorched heart left like a reckless moth.

Don't forget, at the high-class banquet of the just and noble,
the drunk who chuckles to himself over dawn-red wine.

When you flash that smile, radiance glinting like a sapphire cup—
legends pass between me and your ruby lips.

Recall: when the Friend put me on like a belt, how
we rode the new moon like a chariot, circling the earth, in orbit.

Please remember: I may be a drunken wretch, but
what they lack at the mosque I have found in the tavern.

Don't forget: your careful renderings have fixed the gold chain
for the solid pearls of Hafiz.

The Work

Streaming like wind into the street of the Friend, my breath
soaked, saturated... by the fragrance of her braided hair.

Everything I've gained from learning and religion:
so many scattered coins on the dusty road to the beloved.

Minus wine and love, why bother? Life goes by, a waste.
I've had enough. From now on, I set my face to the work.

Where is the morning breeze? Let my beat-up bloody soul be
ransom for a single breath, the fragrance of her braided hair.

Flickering in the breeze, a sun-lit morning candle
I shoulder the welcome load, throw myself into the work.

In honor of that look you flash: I let my life go to ruin—
strengthening the ground of the original promise.

Don't play-act Hafiz, hypocrisy and pretense warp the heart—
far better the path of love, the highroad of abandon.

On the Road to Aiman

Ah, dawn breeze, where is my beloved?
That heart-rending trickster moon, where has she gone?

It's growing dark; on the road ahead lies the valley of Aiman.
Where is the mountain fire, the place to bear witness?

Everyone enters the world stamped with the mark of ruin.
Don't ask in the taverns, 'Where is the wise man now?'

From the ranks of the evangelists, one who can read the signs—
the subtleties are many, where is the keeper of secrets?

With you, the tip of each hair on my head—a masterwork.
Where have we come to? and who would dare reproach us?

Reason is worried. The heart has curled up in a corner; where
is the lock of fragrant hair, the cherished eyebrow of my beloved?

Wine-bringer, vocalist and kegs of wine, all of them are ready—
but the show can't start without the beloved. Where...

Hafiz, don't worry over autumn wind in a fleeting orchard.
Be reasonable; where is there a rose without thorn?

The Tangled Braid

May his radiant light be the Sun of every gaze
and his face held more beautiful than fleeting charms.

May her braid, like a bird of paradise, the royal falcon
keep the heart of rulers safe beneath her wings.

May those not totally entangled in her braid
be twisted and flung about like the braid of the beloved.

May the heart not rapt at the beauty of her face
be consumed by the poison of envy.

When your sly glance fires its arrows
let my punctured heart be the only shield.

Red as rubies, sweet as sugar, when your lips at last grant a kiss…
let my lips never lose the taste of that sweetness.

At every breath a fresh pang of longing…
your loveliness seems to grow by the moment.

Hafiz has given his life to longing for your face—
may you look upon the need of your lovers.

On the Way

There's no shoreline on the way of love,
apart from giving everything you are, no remedy.

Whenever the heart's given over in love: sweetness.
There's no need of approval for doing what is right.

Call the path of drunkenness fruitful leisure, though
like the secret route to a gold-horde, few know the way.

Don't trouble us with Reason's nagging. Bring more wine!
In the counties of the heart, that sheriff has no jurisdiction.

With the eye of the pure one can see him, like the crescent moon.
Not every eye reflects that radiant moonlight.

Ask my gaze, 'Who conquers us!?'
My love, not the sin of fortune, or the crime of a star.

The weeping of Hafiz can't find a path through to you.
Amazed, I find your heart grown hard as granite.

Lack

The moon lacks your radiant face.
Before you, the most exquisite rose lacks splendor.

My heart has curled up in the curve of your brow—
no king has such a delightful niche.

I looked into your stark black eyes,
there was no regard for anyone.

Tavern novice, fill my cup
for wine is like the joy of a care-free master.

Wait! or my smoking heart may scar your face…
the least sigh fogs over that fragile glass.

Hold still and hide your wound, for that delicate heart
can't bear to hear the pleas of her lovers.

I'm not the only one struck by your stark black tress.
Could anyone *not* be marked by its beauty?

Behold her bold eyes budding open before you—
the ardent gaze lacks all discretion.

Say to those with no way through to the beloved:
Soak your sleeve in the well of jealousy.

Don't censor Hafiz if he bows down before you,
the infidel of Love is free from sin.

Surrender

Bringer of wine, pass around the cup, be lavish!
for love that seemed easy at first turned out to be full of struggle.

Ah, the blood flooding into our hearts
when the breeze spread the fragrance of her braid...

At the master's command, soak your prayer-mat with purple wine.
Every traveler knows the road and the customs of the journey.

At camp, in the caravan of the fair one, how can I rest?
Each moment the bell cries, 'Load the camels!'

Horrid darkness—dread—the sucking vortex—
what can light-weights strolling the shore ever know of our state?

In the end, my work brought me nothing but a bad reputation—
and yet how its power endures, known to the faithful.

Hafiz, if you want the beloved near, draw near yourself,
let go of the world when you come to her, surrendering all.

Stung

As the wine merchant cares for the needs of the drunk
God forgives sin, and wards off pestilence.

Bringer of wine, be fair and fill up the poor man's cup
so his craving won't spill over and fill the world with grief.

For those of us stung by loss and craving wine
either fine wine or reunion will remedy our pain.

And yet, from these sufferings, the word of peace may come
if the pilgrim stays devoted to the covenant of faith.

Seeker, should toil come to you, or rest,
trace these to no one else; both have come from God.

In sweatshops where there's no room for thought or understanding
why do the ignorant make needless work?

Singer, strum the lute: 'No one perished before his time.'
Whoever doesn't hum along is sadly ignorant.

Wasted with desire for wine, Hafiz was scorched by love—
where is the breath of Jesus, to raise us back to life?

Snared

The wrecked heart has snared itself in your braided hair…
Slay it with a glance! a heart so trapped deserves it.

If your hand should give what our heart desires…
pour it into our hands, your gift its own reward.

Such a rose doesn't need exotic perfumes
but keeps a stash of fragrance deep in its pocket.

Ah, beloved, in the dark night alone
I burn myself up like a blazing candle.

I warned you songbird, at your first glimpse of love:
Watch out! the rose stands alone and won't be moved.

Forget the cheap lords of this passing world—
the treasure of your soul is a palace of its own.

Scorched to the core, Hafiz continues to flirt and tease
but in keeping the covenant he's fidelity itself.

Scorched

Lost to sight, I offer you to God.
You scorched my soul—its ashes hold you beloved.

Until I've wrapped the shroud around myself in death
I will not let go of your robe.

Show the curved prayer-niche of your eyebrow, until
I raise my hand at dawn to caress your neck.

If I have to cut deals with the gods of Babylon, so be it:
whatever black magic it takes, to make you return.

Faithless healer, I want to die with you near me.
Come check on your patient again, I wait for you with longing.

I have wept rivers, turned my eyes into a wellspring
hoping to sow in your heart the seed of love.

It's not like you Hafiz, these drunken erotic escapades…
though, should you fall apart completely, all is forgiven.

Loss in Translation

Not all the beautiful know the art of stealing hearts,
not all princes can mirror Alexander.

Not all regal dandies know the way to wear
a crown, the customs and laws of a sovereign.

Don't work for pay like a beggar,
the Friend knows how to reward his slaves.

Done well, fidelity to the covenant is blessing—
done poorly it becomes oppression.

I risked all, madly in love, not knowing:
she was mortal but skilled in miraculous tricks.

I would serve that crazy drunk—burning up,
he dressed like a beggar though a master alchemist.

A thousand fine hairs are woven in this thread:
Not everyone who shaves their head is a dervish.

My rapt eyes circle the mole of my beloved,
for the rare jewel's known only to the jeweler.

A beautiful king may rule the beautiful.
If he acts with justice he can seize the world.

Only those schooled in the art of Persian eloquence
fully know the yearning in Hafiz' poems.

Cracked

Last night we passed around the legend of your tress
remembering all through the night the chain of your braided hair.

Though my heart gushed blood, struck by the arrow of your eyelash
I never stopped longing for the bow of your brow.

The wind brought word from you—blessings upon it!
Who else could sneak into your secret neighborhood?

The fierce ache of yearning was unknown on the earth
until a wink of your eye caused a worldwide panic.

Cracked in the head, I used to be among the upright—
the curl of your braid was the snare on my path.

Loosen the knot of your robe, so my heart may be opened as well
for all release and openness have come to me from you.

Keeping your vow, pass by the grave of Hafiz
for he fled from the world, longing for your face.

Daydreams

Stupid accuser, mind your own business. Why the uproar?
My heart's wandering lost in the paths of love—what happened to yours?

If her lips won't give me the kiss I long for, all the advice in the world
will blow right through me like wind through a flute.

The One made from nothing, the waist of the beloved
holds a riddle no creature can hope to solve.

The beggar on your street depends on nothing in the universe
and your slave is completely free of this world and the next.

Wasted, falling down drunk with love…and yet
my heart's foundations are that ruined metropolis.

O heart, don't whine about the harshness of the Friend,
his justice has measured out what is fitting.

Enough with the raving fantasies and daydreams
Hafiz, we've heard it all before—give us the real thing!

Bloodshot

If the fair ones remain so seductive
they might crack the armor of the orthodox.

Wherever the flowering Branch might bloom
the gaze of his lovers becomes the ground.

Superb Virtuoso—when he starts to play
the holy ones dance and wave their hands.

Young friend, upright cypress: Hit that ball!
before the game makes your upright posture its club.

Lovers have no self-control,
whatever you command, they do.

Eyes bloodshot with constant longing…
where is there greater injustice and grief?

Compared to my streaming eyes
Noah's flood…a mere raindrop.

When can we feast our eyes on your face
so your lovers can offer their souls in sacrifice.

Set forth O heart, grief or not—the wise
can live at ease in the mix of love and loss.

Hafiz, don't turn away from late night grief
until your daybreak shines like a mirror.

Sacked and Plundered

At daybreak the breeze carried a faint perfume, the fragrant hair of the beloved
sweeping my anxious heart into the new day, awake and ready for work.

From the wrecked garden of my heart I tore out form like a fir-tree
for all the flowers tended by its love bore fruit that was hard and bitter.

Afraid to be sacked and plundered by love I let my heart bleed
but in gushing forth there was no escape, and it was ravaged.

When the sun blazed at the peak of its castle battlements
the moon turned away, face to the wall in shame.

Whenever wine arrived, or poems, I followed their call
for the roads were poor then, and often, the courier could not make it through.

First and last, the path of grace and beauty is the gift of the beloved
whether fingering beads, or knotting the cord of a sacred belt.

I was amazed to see Hafiz last night with a full cup of wine…
but I didn't complain, he behaved like a genuine Sufi.

Forgive, Lord, the wrinkle of his eyebrow. Although it left me helpless
its seductive play brought comfort to my yearning heart.

The Secret of the Work

I yearn for you each night. I'm getting desperate... *Your suffering will end.*
Be the moon of my wretched heart. *If the moon should rise, I will be.*

Learn the way of faith from lovers.
Even the rising moon can't teach you the secret of the work.

I look at you and turn away, put up roadblocks between your image and
      my greedy look. But it's no use.
My image travels the back roads and arrives at night, by another road.

The fragrance of your hair left me lost and stranded.
Breathe that scent in deeper and what gets you lost will be your guide.

Spring morning. The smell of wet earth in the garden of the Beautiful...
Calm and warm, the faint breeze drifting from a nearby street,
      the home of the beloved.

To drink from your lips... just once... I want to kiss you so bad it kills me.
Give over everything to Love. He honors those who become his slave.

When will your merciful love set everything right?
Until the day comes, keep silence. Don't say a thing, to anyone.

Did you not see? Our time together, all our delight: faded.
Hafiz, be quiet. This bitter loss will also end.

A Drop of Rain

Hafiz the lonely hermit went out last night to the tavern
travelled from the calm of promise to the ecstasy of the cup.

Young, fresh, the beloved came to him in sleep and
though an old man at night, he woke up delirious with love.

The monk who yesterday smashed both bottle and cup
today, with one slug of wine, regained his wisdom.

Everyone fell in love with that fresh young novice and
followed after him; where he disappeared to, no one knows.

The torch of the rose devoured the field of nightingales—
the giddy flicker of the candle-flame: the moth's destruction.

Weeping—at daybreak, at nightfall, grateful that it's not mere loss,
each rain drop will become a radiant jewel.

The gaze of the bringer of wine spoke such bewitching scriptures
the drudgery of evening prayer became a festival of song.

At last Hafiz has entered the inmost court of the King,
his heart has returned to its keeper, his life to its source.

The Orchard of Delight

There's a lush garden of paradise in the monk's bare cell,
his secret work is a fountain of gracious power.

The gold-hoard of loneliness, its marvels and talismans,
starts with a merciful gaze from the Sufi's broken heart.

In the castle on the other side, through a door to the inmost garden:
the orchard of delight, where the dervish, bearing witness, whirls.

Dull lead changed into purest gold by the radiant light of God
such is the sweet alchemy in the friendship of the holy ones.

The glory before which the sun lays down its crown in praise
such is the noble strength in the courtesy of the dervish.

Though the army of Sin reaches from shore to shore,
from before to after-eternity, the triumph of the poor ones.

Beyond loss, and the grief that haunts all things that fade, without
fuss or elaborate ritual, the monk guards the treasure of his heart.

Snatched from the hand of the poor, the horded wealth of Qarun
makes the zeal of the dervish burn.

O big shot politician, don't boast of your fleeting fame! Your fate
depends on the secret hope nourished in the heart of monks.

The face of the longed-for beloved, sought by kings in prayer,
shines in the clear mirror of the dervish-life.

My patron's like a modern day Asef, right-hand man to the king.
His protective gaze shares the wisdom of the dervishes.

Hafiz! on the edge of eternal day, drink that purest water of life
whose wellspring is a speck of dust on the floor of the poor one's cell.

The Sultan's Crown

A brief second spent grieving her loss is worth more than all the world.
Sell your sufi-robe for wine, it's good for nothing else.

The wine-dealers won't do business; whatever I have,
the prayer-mat of my stern devotions...isn't worth a cup.

The gate-keeper turned me away; what's happened
that I'm not worth the dust on your doorstep?

The sultan's crown holds the power of life and death—
it's attractive, sure, but not worth risking your head.

How easy it seemed at first, sailing the flood in quest of treasure...
Now, I wouldn't leave shore for a thousand pearls.

Better you should hide your face from your lovers,
the joy of victory's not worth the trouble of keeping captives.

In free surrender, struggle on like Hafiz, forgetting the world...
even if the least seed of effort should repay your weight in gold.

Glitter

A famous courier from the land of the Friend
brought a talisman of life... and scriptures soaked with His fragrance.

He gave an eloquent sign of God's strength and beauty
awakening our hope...in the hope-filled heart of the Friend.

I paid for his word with my heart...but I'm a bit embarrassed:
it's not much of a trade, the few scattered coins of my self in exchange for the Friend.

Thanks be to God! all the work of Providence
conspires to make known his love for us.

Traveling sky, cycling moon—what choice do they have?
they circle according to the plan and free desire of the Friend.

Should the wind of the End Times slam together this world and the next, shattering all,
you'll find me in the ruined street, watching for the Friend.

Dawn breeze, bring me crushed jewels, glitter to mix with mascara...
from the dust of the fortunate road where the Friend has walked.

When the enemy spouts off against Hafiz—so what?
In the presence of the Friend I am free of shame.

Every Morning, Wind

Over night the wind brought word: the Friend has arrived at last—
I give my heart to the wind and whatever may come so be it.

My work reached a point where friends were let in on the secret:
each night the flash of lightning, and every morning, wind.

Buried in the curl of your braid, my defenseless heart
has not thought once of what it left behind.

Now I see the power in the guidance of the holy ones,
O Lord, make the soul of our master rejoice.

My heart pumps blood through the memory of you every
moment: how, in the dark garden, the night wind loosened
        the rose-bud knot of your robe...

Crushed, desolate, strength slipped out of my drooping hand...
a cool dawn wind, the hope of your love gave it back again.

Hafiz, your noble heart will in time reach the end of longing—
if lives must be lost in ransom, it's worth the cost.

A Handful of Sand

Those who look out for his faithful friends,
God looks out for them, guarding them in trials.

If you want the beloved not to break his promise
keep your part of the bargain; he will keep his.

I speak my longing for the friend to the friend alone.
Who else could stand guard over this deep conversation?

Heart, head, life, money: ransom to the beloved
who guards the heart of friendship, our covenant of love.

Morning wind, if you see my heart dangling from the tress of the beloved,
be gracious and tell it to stay where it is!

My heart, live in such a way that if your footsteps falter
an angel, his hands already spread out in prayer, an angel may bear you up.

It seems like he let me slip…but there's no place for indignation.
What good is a wretched slave? In the end he'll take care of me.

Keep a handful of sand from your backstreet, that Hafiz
may hold in memory the freshness of the morning breeze.

The Book of Delight

From before eternal day, the radiance of your beauty breathed forth glory—
Love has shown his face, spreading fire throughout the universe.

Love has shown his face—he saw when the angel grew envious,
how, from the smoldering contagious flame, all of us caught fire.

The lamp of the mind craved to glow with that infectious flame.
It struck the earth like lightning, and from that first spark of envy: wars, famine, hatred.

The accuser bore witness in the court of Beauty,
but its radiance struck him down like an unseen hand.

Others sought the life of ease and contentment.
Tried by grief, our hearts alone chose the way of love, and sorrow.

The pure soul yearned for a glimpse of her dimpled chin
and to bury his hands in her lavish curls.

When he cast aside the pleasures of the self-content
Hafiz made a book of delight in your love.

Plunder

Plant the tree of friendship that blossoms as the heart's desire,
tear up the seedling of malice, that only bears fruit in sorrow.

Be courteous with those at the tavern
tomorrow may find you hung-over and craving more.

Our brief time together, like the plunder of a desperate war—
the sun will trace many circles before another chance like this one.

The one who bears the litter of Layla takes charge of the cradle of the moon.
Place upon his heart, O God, to carry it past Majnun.

Yearn, heart, for interior spring. Each year the orchard explodes
in roses: lavish as wildflowers…or nightingales.

For God's sake—when the punctured heart makes a deal with your tress
tell that brilliant Jewel to put my soul at peace.

As an old man Hafiz may again God-willing reach the garden
and sit by the stream, in the shade of his cypress.

Sleepless

The day of favor has dawned at last, the sun a cup of fire—
what could be a better moment? Pass the cup of wine.

There was peace in the house, the Friend played host, the vocalist spoke with eloquence.
It was a rare season of luxury, a time of wine, and youth.

Delight in the whole creation, joy in its ecstatic beauty,
like purple wine in a crafted goblet of beaten gold.

Combing creation's hair, the cosmic Beautician daydreamed of the finest wine,
drew sweet perfume from the petals of the rose.

Falling-down drunk, the beloved and the vocalist reeled about dancing.
The gaze of the Friend had stolen sleep from the bleary eyes of the revelers.

Should the moon buy the pearls of Hafiz, each moment
the melody of lutes would reach to the ear of Venus.

Fever

The night has come, the Night of Power as the holy ones have told us...
Lord, what constellation makes this night so full of blessing?

That no sacrilegious hand should caress your braid
the holy ones form a circle, remembering your Name.

One glimpse and I'm swallowed by the well of your dimpled chin...
multitudes bend their necks to the yoke of adoration.

Galloping through space, my lord, his face like the mirror of a radiant moon...
the peak of the sun, dust under the horseshoe of his mount.

At the glistening sweat on her naked cheek, the sun
seized by yearning burns with fever every day.

I have no desire to leave the full cup of wine or the Friend.
To those who abstain: Sorry, these are my rule of life.

The arrow of her glance has punctured my heart,
the power of Hafiz' life in the secret of her kiss.

Like a stream from the beak of a crow, living water
flows from the tip of my pen—blessed wellspring!

Return

O Lord, return that tender fawn to Khutan,
let that fair and taunting cypress come back to the orchard.

Breathe softly on our worn-out hearts like a flutist,
return the lost soul to its body.

Sun and moon assume their place at your command—
make the friend, with her moon-like face, return to me as well.

Hunting for the Yemeni jewel with bloodshot eyes—
return that glorious star, Lord, to Yemen.

Regal bird of the ancient way, with the words of mere crows
and sparrows, fly before the Holy Dove.

The word is out: who could want life without you?
Listen, beloved messenger: share the news, return the word.

May the one who belongs in the loving gaze of Hafiz
return from the wasteland to his native place.

Shot from the Bow

Wine-drunk, bottle in hand, my friend stormed into the temple—
a glance from his beaming eyes and all the drinkers in the crowd were blasted.

High on his noble mount, one horseshoe catching a ray of light
from the slender moon, he towered over ancient fir-trees.

Say, if you like, of the self: 'It is'; or if you prefer: 'It's not';
My rapt gaze fixed on the beloved, what difference does it make?

When the friend rose to leave, the candle of our one heart melted.
When he sat back down: a glad murmuring among his lovers.

The beloved's fragrant hair, the source of every sweet perfume
and the bow of indigo dye followed the curve of her eyebrow.

Come back! So the sad life of Hafiz may come back as well...
though the arrow once shot from the bow, does not return.

Reading by the Light of Your Face

Last night our Master went from the mosque to the tavern.
Pious friends, what can we do but follow?

From the Day of Alast it's been promised:
in the taverns of the wise we shall also take our place.

Full of yearning, how can we turn our face to the shrine
when the Master has set his face to the tavern?

Our night-long sighs, the ferocious blaze of desire…
will anything melt his frozen heart?

If the wise knew the bliss of those tangled in her braid
following its weave would make their heads spin.

The wind blew your hair in my face and the world went dark—
superb shelter! no grace of your braid could surpass this gift.

We laid a snare for the bird of prey, the heart's falcon—
but you let down your hair and the bird escaped.

The gracious light of your face revealed the sacred page to us—
our every gloss now glistens with light and joy.

Our sighs like arrows launched beyond the atmosphere of Earth—
careful Hafiz, you might get shot!

The World of Care

Hurry! In the palace of hope, the corner-stone is cracking…
And don't forget the wine—for all life is built on wind.

Driven by a thirst for the summit, under the naked sky
my heart's free from every trace of entanglement.

How can I explain? falling-down drunk at the wine-house…
From an envoy of the unseen, what joyful news!

Falcon, perch high in the Lote-tree, at the edge of what man can know
and not in the dank back alleys of a world that is passing fast.

From the highest peak of the celestial throne, they cry,
'What's happened to you, trapped in this net of shades?'

From the master of my own path, a word of counsel,
assimilate this truth before you bring it forth in practice:

Don't seek as faithful wife, this shifty adulterous world—
the old hag is the promised bride of a thousand desperate suitors.

Don't brood over a fading world, and take my words to heart,
they were a counsel of love to me, from a wise fellow traveler:

Glad for what you've received, loosen the knot of your forehead—
to such as you and I, the door of choice is closed.

There is no sure promise of faithful love in the smile of a fading rose.
Weep like the plaintive nightingale, the world is a place of sorrow.

O second-rate versifiers, why be envious of Hafiz?
a tranquil heart and eloquent speech are gifts of God alone.

The Falcon

Remember how I dwelt at the gate to your street—
my radiant gaze grew from the dust on your doorstep.

From life in good company—the rose, the iris—
my tongue learned to speak the secrets of your heart.

As the heart murmured lines from the master of wisdom
Love spoke, loosening its tangled knots.

Inscribed on my heart: Never live without the friend.
How has all my strength proved futile?

Last night, to honor old friends, I drank hard in every tavern.
Wine in the bottle, blood in the heart …awakening, my head on the pavement.

I have traveled for years seeking a reason for the pain of loss,
but reason in such a case means nothing.

Surely, the turquoise seal of the King
sparkled… but its beauty was passing fast.

Did you see, Hafiz, the smirk of that arrogant partridge?
How blind he was to the falcon, the grasping talons of destiny.

Love's Arsenal

Like a noose, the curve of your braid catches pious and unbeliever—
only one of many weapons in the arsenal of Love.

Your beauty contains the shock of all loveliness,
the mere rumor of your teasing wink: complete enchantment.

How could any soul escape your seductive glance—
that look, with the bow of your eyebrow, lurking in ambush.

A hundred blessings on the dark eyes of the beloved—
the way they assassinate lovers is a magic art.

To know love's innumerable faces is a wisdom
stretching from the core of Earth to the edge of the universe.

Don't think that speaker of evil can escape without punishment,
he will have to face those who record each word.

Hafiz, don't think you're safe from the snare of her braid—
having stolen your heart, she's after your religion!

No Word

It's been far too long since I heard from the keeper of my heart…
not a word, not a single 'peace be with you.'

I've sent a hundred letters, and he, with all his retinue,
hasn't dispatched one courier, with a single word;

Not the elegant leaping deer nor the arrogant partridge…
The last scrap of my reason

like a bird about to fly out of my hand—
not a glimpse of his face to keep me grounded.

My sweet-talking friend, a drunk himself,
knew I was craving for wine and would not send a cup.

I used to boast of our intimate union—
now he won't even speak to me.

Hafiz, don't lose your cool. If the King
doesn't call for his slave: so be it.

This and That

From the same Friend: the deep ache of loneliness, and healing balm.
I've promised him my body and my inmost soul.

They say This, '*That* is better than beauty'—
but This and That alike belong to the Friend.

What I have murmured beneath the veil
will be cried out loud in the streets as well.

In the one beam of light from his radiant face: This world and That—
words, straightforward yet supremely indirect.

Remember the One who, hunting us down, bound to avenge
broke his promise like a braided tress.

There's no sure foothold in this changing world,
still less on the circling spheres.

Though the treasure of our time had to come to an end
the days of separation will also pass.

Both The Police Force of True Religion and the right hand man
of the king know Hafiz as an ardent lover.

What do lovers care about the government? bring more wine,
(and forget about the rules of the Sultan, too).

Seduced

He took my heart then hid his face.
God! how could anyone endure this game?

Almost dawn; seduced by loneliness
thoughts of you flood my heart, a shore-less ocean.

Why is my heart not streaked with blood like a tulip?
for his proud eye will not look down to my need.

Sick with yearning…how can I say this?
The healer has put my life at risk.

So devoured—a wax candle by His searing flame—
that the wine-bottle wept in sympathy and the lute began to moan.

Dawn wind, if you know the cure, now's the time—
relentless desire has seduced my heart.

How can I explain to my friends
that Love itself said one thing and did something else.

It's not Hafiz' enemy that's done this
but the glance of the Friend, shot from the bow of his eyebrow.

Strangers

So many seekers of your unseen face—
the vision, still in bud, throbs with promise.

Although I'm far from you (telling myself, No one should be far from you),
I burn with hope: soon we'll be together.

If I appear on your doorstep, don't be surprised,
like me, many strangers and exiles seek your land.

What lover has not been touched by the glance of the Friend?
Surely, there is no pain, and where there is pain, a gracious Healer.

Monastery, tavern…in love, it makes no difference—
the radiant face of the Friend shines everywhere on earth.

The monks at their work show forth glory
in the word of the Cross, their rule of life.

Hafiz bears witness: in the end, everything is not in vain—
a fabulous myth and an amazing word.

The Road to Iraq

Remember him—though he forgot us and left without warning
or the least farewell to comfort our wretched hearts.

Eternally young, author of peace and goodness
why not liberate your worn-out slave?

I soak the paper-thin silk of my robe in bloody water
for the sky won't show me the path to the banner of his justice.

My heart, hoping its voice might reach to you, cried out across
the mountains—not even Farhad made such a cry.

When your shadow passed out of the orchard, the morning-bird
could not build its nest in the branches of your braided hair.

Show the dawn-wind, your courier, how to do its job—
there's no force swifter than you, the master of speed itself.

The bride's beautician could not produce what he wished—
so with those who put no faith in his beauty.

Poet, change your song, set out on the road to Iraq
for the Friend set out on this path…and left no trace.

Iraqi songs belong to Hafiz, roads that
scorch the heart—take them and you won't complain.

Morning Prayer

I'm the sort who lives in the corner of the tavern,
my ritual prayer at dawn: the secret words of the Sage.

If I don't hear the song of the harp at dawn... so what?
the music of my groaning justifies my love.

Praise God I'm free of the entire net, beggar to sultan—
the poor wretch at the door of the Friend is my only King.

From the mosque to the tavern, all I want is our union—
with God as my witness, I have no other hope.

From the moment I lay my face on your doorstep
I've taken my rest above the throne of the sun.

With the sword of Fate, I might cut the ropes of my tent free—
if not, I'll stay and fight; it's not in my nature to run.

Hafiz, although it was not our choice to sin,
still, play along, and continue to say 'We sinned'.

Words on the Heart

I have seen the light of God in the taverns of the wise—
Behold the radiance, amazed: where does it come from?

Don't boast to me about your pilgrimage. You
see a house, I see the true house of God.

I would open the pouch of incense in the idol's sacred braid—
Don't imagine what I found was sinful.

Blazing heart, streaming eyes, the first hint of dawn, a wail in the night:
all of these at once in your loving gaze.

With each breath remembering the image of your face—
How could I tell what I see on the inmost screen of my heart?

No one has known such luxuriant perfume
as I've found each day on the morning breeze.

Friends, don't censor Hafiz for his flirtatious gaze,
I can see he's among your true lovers.

Gone

I craved the taste of your lips, like a drink, like finest wine
but a glimpse of your moonlike face, and that was it, you were gone...

He can't stand us anymore, I don't know why.
He packed his bags and left. Before we'd even arrived, he was gone.

It may be we scared him off with all our prayer—
chanting, fasts and ritual around the clock...but he was already gone.

His glance said, I never leave the path of longing...
and we fell for it, we started after him... but he was gone.

Gracious, elegant, gliding through the morning orchard,
he was far beyond us; we tried to catch up... he was gone.

We groaned and sighed for days, keening like Hafiz—but it was
no use. Farewell, beloved! long before we arrived, you were gone.

Insurrection

Who will bring my prayer to the courtiers of the Sultan:
'Grateful at your power, don't send the beggar from your gaze.'

The devil's forever on the lookout—I trust myself to God—
for his sake maybe that brilliant star will help.

If the dagger of your eyelash should threaten to slit our throats…
be careful O heart—no sudden moves…

You scorch the world's heart with the light of your face.
What do you have to gain that you're so relentless?

I hope each night that the word of friends
on the morning breeze may please the Friend.

What a superb insurrection you reveal to your lovers!
For a glimpse of your face we cast our lives before you.

For God's sake, a bit of wine for Hafiz!
so his prayer at dawn wins blessing for us all.

On the Path

When you drink that wine, sprinkle some on the dusty path.
Why trouble yourself over a fault that brings good to others?

Go along, with whatever you have; drink deeply and banish grief
for the ruthless sword of the world will strike without remorse.

O my spoiled delicate cypress! by the dust of your slender foot,
on the final Day, do not stand far from the dust of my body.

Hellish or celestial, human or sublime, all the great doctrines
acknowledge: there is one path of impiety, the refusal to give.

Architect of the far horizon, the mathematics of the path leave
no way out of the cosmic labyrinth.

Delicious wine splashed over the path of Reason—
may the vineyard flourish 'til the final Day!

Hafiz, in bliss, on the way to the wine-house, you left the world.
May the poor ones' prayer stay close to your heart.

Niche

Bold, heroic, the gold horizon-light floods the bare table of those who fast.
The slim crescent of a feast-day moon looks up at us and winks
          circling the rim of the wine-cup.

A glimpse of the dust on the floor of Love's wine-house counts
for more than a ritual pilgrimage and the rigorous month-long fast.

My primordial home: the dark back corner of the tavern.
May God deal richly with the builders of this holy place!

The curved eyebrow of the beloved like a prayer-niche in the local mosque
where the truly pious are washed in the blood of the inmost heart.

That ruby-colored wine, how much? It will cost the jewel of your reason.
But don't worry—those who have made the deal came out on top.

Ah, what a shame; for once (bad conscience?) the elder looked down
on our Sufi reveling, as we knocked back the dregs from the wine-cup.

Forget the slick rhetoric of these righteous preachers, however polished,
and hear the true word of love from Hafiz.

The Lantern

Bringer of wine, come! for the Friend has removed the veil from his face,
and in the empty cell, the dried-out lantern is lit once more.

The cut wick of the wax candle, the face of its lopped-off head, is lit again
as the worn-out master has raised his head a fresh and brazen youth.

Love gave a seductive wink and fear of the Lord veered from the path…
the Friend so attractive his enemies had no escape.

Careful! his gracious eloquence can charm the heart—
his pistachio-red lips turn speech into sugar.

When the harsh load of grief cut into our hearts,
one with the breath of Jesus removed our burden and healed our wound.

The virgins whose beauty outshone the moon and sun…
as soon as you appeared they were out of work.

The story of your grace ripples and spreads through the universe—
only the most short-sighted would try to cut it short.

O Hafiz, where did you learn such holy and prayerful eloquence
so that Destiny has made your words a talisman, etching them in gold.

Morning Wine

Now that the rose has arisen from nothingness into the orchard
the violet bows down at its feet.

Plaintive drum, strumming harp—down a cup of wine at dawn.
Flute-song and plangent lute—kiss the one who brings the cup.

In the shifting seasons of the rose, stay near to the beloved, to the harp, and wine,
for the time of such pleasures is fleeting.

Rivaling heaven, the earth has grown lush with fragrant shrubs, towering forests...
blessed by luck and a fortunate star.

From the hand of the fair beloved, whose breath, like Jesus', wakes the dead,
receive the cup of wine; forget the stock prophecies of doom and destruction.

In the reign of the rose and the lily, the earth became like heaven.
So what? all such sweetness is fleeting.

At dawn, the rose was carried on the breeze like Solomon...
and birdsong began, like the melodies of David.

Grow faith in the garden of the world like Abraham
before devotion to the gods of Nimrod spreads like a fire.

Drink a dawn toast to the noble counselor,
the minister of Solomon, and Column of Religion.

May the circle of Hafiz prosper
and whatever they seek come to pass.

Learning by Heart

The pompously orthodox, showing off at prayer, in the pulpit,
act otherwise in their inner room.

I have just one question. Ask the circle of the wise:
Why don't the preachers of repentance change their own ways?

You might think, They scorn the day of judgment,
when you see how shamefully *they* judge.

I've become the glad slave of the tavern's master whose carefree
wandering monks toss dust on the treasures of the world.

Boasting of their mules and slave-boys…
Put these donkey-sellers back in their place!

O messenger of God, at the door of Love's tavern, praise him!
For there they make the leaven of Adam's clay rise like fermenting dough.

His supreme beauty lops the heads off innumerable lovers
and yet, out of nowhere, more of them raise their heads.

O beggar at the common sufi-lodge…come on! In the dwelling of the wise
they will give you a drink and set you free.

O heart, empty out your house, so the King can find a home,
for the proud have made of their heart a battlefield of clashing armies.

Dawn—a great cry from the celestial Throne:
Everyone in heaven's learning the poems of Hafiz by heart!

The Seed of Courage

The plaintive words of Jacob:
Loss of the beloved cannot be said.

The terrifying sermon on the End
spoke in shadows of loss and the beloved.

Where can I find a trace of the Friend?
The morning wind served as courier but garbled his speech.

Faithless, unlovely moon, betrayer of the Friend
how easily you spoke of leaving our circle.

Stunned by loss, I stand before God, thankful...
my heart has grown strong in suffering, unafraid of pain.

The wind itself told Solomon: Don't tie your hopes
to the wind, even when it blows your way.

Don't leave the path for the scrap of ease offered by the World.
Since when has that wretched hag abandoned her gossip?

Fend off sorrow with drink, devouring Time and care.
In the words of the wise farmer: Wine is the seed of courage.

Don't quibble over this and that; the wise servant
welcomes the words of lovers at every moment.

Who says Hafiz thinks of you no longer?
A slanderous lie! may it never be so.

Torn and Stained

Their gaze turns dust into gold—
May they blink in my direction.

Hide your need from accusing doctors,
a remedy may yet arrive from the storehouse of the Invisible.

When the beloved won't remove the veil from his face,
why do people dream up such fantasies?

Since the beauty of the world to come lies beyond both
drunkenness and abstinence, trust everything to grace.

Never leave knowledge of God. In the excess of love
the knowers do business with those they know.

Drink up! better a hundred sins behind the veil
than the open worship of hypocrites.

The coat-of-many-colors, fragrant with my Joseph
was torn and stained by the envious.

In this life, crimes and outrage are done behind the veil.
What will happen when the veil is torn?

When the hard rock weeps at my eloquence, don't be surprised;
the master speaks words from deep in the heart.

Hafiz, there's no easy way to lasting union,
Kings rarely condescend to beggars.

Highway Robbery

There's no one in this city who can bear away my heart.
With luck, fate may pack my bags and carry me off.

Where is the friend, noble, drunk, before whose generous love
my ravished heart can bare its deepest yearning.

Sad gardener, I see you know nothing of the fall to come
when the most exquisite rose will freeze in the wind.

Keep alert! Time, like a roadside bandit, will never rest—
what he hasn't carried off today, he may tomorrow.

I daydream so often, the one who has captured my gaze
may come to dream of me likewise.

Forty years my heart has stored all the knowledge and grace it could
and yet in one glance she may carry it off as plunder.

The lowing of the golden calf...don't be duped by its seductive call!
What idolater competes with the miracles of Moses?

The wine-cup alone keeps the heart from narrowing,
never let it go—or the flood of sadness may carry you off.

Walk the path of love with care; though it's
the hunting-ground of archers, you'll carry off their prize.

Hafiz, if the seductive wink of the friend should track you down,
clear out—surrender your house, that he may take possession.

Ambush

Dark complexion, wine-colored eyes, half-smile
on a radiant face—all the bliss of the universe.

The fair and eloquent may be truly the rulers of the world
but there's only one Solomon with the seal of power.

The secret grain of the wheat-colored mole on the cheek
of the beloved was the bandit that ambushed Adam.

My beloved plans to leave—friends, for God's sake, help!
What will I do with my shattered heart when the one who can heal it is gone?

In a clean robe, masterful, with shining face...
the fair ones of this world and the next both seek him.

Who could grasp the riddle: the one who has hardened his heart to our prayer
has struck us down... with the breath of Jesus, son of Mary.

Hafiz is truly orthodox, hold him in honor!
for he forgives everyone, and knows they are blessed.

Eclipse

Your face lights the traveler's every path
and the fragrant breeze of your hair—saturates our hearts.

Against accusers who condemn our love
our one defense: the gracious beauty of your face.

Listen! the sweet apple of your dimpled chin says,
A thousand Josephs have fallen in our well.

If my hand drew back from your offered lock of hair
I would sin by stinginess and waste at once.

Say to the doorman guarding the inmost room,
Move over; I too am a beggar in the court of God.

Though veiled from the gaze of our mortal eyes
he is held forever in the gaze of the tranquil heart.

If, as an old man, Hafiz should knock on the door: Open up!
for years now he's yearned for our moonlike face.

The Breath of Jesus

What a gift! the sweat of your pen recorded our every act of love...
all destined for reward by your generous grace.

With the fine tip of your pen you inscribed the sign for 'peace' to me.
May the sweatshop of life in Time never be without such writings.

It's no accident you remembered me, your poor one;
surely, your pen never wavers.

Don't let me thank you *too* much for this blessing:
that grateful we may praise you for the gift of gratefulness.

Come closer that I may swear by the tip of your braid:
even if I lose my head it will stay prostrate at your feet.

You will come to know of our yearning (too late!)
when the tulips bloom on the grave of your lovers.

The dawn breeze spoke of your tress to every single rose—
since when did the guards let such seductive couriers into the garden?

Struck to the heart—but how can you grieve... when constantly
they bring you drink from the cup of the very Sultan.

My heart has set up camp at your door; O heart, be grateful!
God has drawn you near.

May your name be fragrant, you with the breeze like Jesus—
for the soul of Hafiz, heart-sore, sprang to life at your breath.

Shelter

Those fixed in longing on the face of the Friend
will never swerve from the circle of his love.

I will rise from the dust of the grave like a tulip,
its black inner core the mark of my yearning.

Rare, singular Jewel—where *are* you?
Grieving you, the world wept oceans.

From the tip of each eyelash, vast floods of water—
Come, I can show you the river.

Like my naked heart, emerge from beneath the veil—
who knows when we might meet again?

Let the shadow of your braid play across my head
that my heart may find rest in its shade.

So proud of heart, you won't even *look* at Hafiz…
but then, indifference is the mark of the beautiful.

Beneath the Veil

Keep your horoscopes, they won't get me closer to the mouth of the Friend.
All the power on earth could not force a way to that inmost secret.

I'd lay down my life anytime for a single taste of her lips...
it's a favor that, somehow, she gives and withholds at once.

I burn away with yearning and, beneath the veil, there is no way out...
or there may be a way, and the holder of the veil won't let me know it.

The dawn breeze tugged vaguely at her tangled hair.
In a dull, miserable world, I crave the windstorm.

As long as I circle the edge, like a compass, a disconnected point,
the vagaries of time will not stop blocking my path to the centre.

Sure, with perseverance, I could get my hands on sugar,
but the broken promise of Time hurries me on.

Let me sleep, I said, I'll see the image of the Friend in slumber;
but Hafiz keeps me up all night with his groaning.

The Work of Love

Blaze, heart, for your burning works rare achievements
and midnight prayer repels a hundred tribulations.

Suffer the Friend's reproach as a lover,
one sly wink atones for every separation.

From earth to heaven the veil is torn
revealing all for the servants of the chalice.

Love, the healer, is considerate and kind, but
if he doesn't find the wound of love how can he work his cure?

Give over your work to God and be glad of heart—
though the enemy is merciless, God is full of compassion.

My luck keeps dozing off…though the one awake may
offer up prayer at dawn in my place.

Burning up, Hafiz lacks the fragrance in the braid of the friend—
perhaps the dawn wind may help change his luck.

The Daughter of the Grape

Friends, the daughter of the grape has thrown aside her veil
and gone to the orthodox police for approval.

She stepped into our circle from behind the screen. Let her
catch her breath, she'll tell the secret of why she stayed away so long.

There, veiled for so long, bound now by the knot of union
she'll become 'the daughter of drunkenness.'

O heart, share the good news! your fellow singer of love
has revealed the path of drunkenness and healed our craving.

Don't be surprised if the rose of my nature bloomed in your breeze
for the bird drew joy from the fragrant rose-leaf.

All the flames, all the waters on earth could not wash out the purple
when the sufi-robe has once been stained by wine.

Hafiz, stay humble, for Satan, the proudly envious, has founded
the world on illusion: wealth, power, love and religion.

Living Water

What sweetness could equal friendship, leisure, the garden in spring?
Call the bringer of wine—why keep us waiting?

Guard the sweetness that comes to you as plunder won from Time.
When everything is passing fast, why hold on?

The joints and sinews of life are held together by a flimsy thread—
swallow your grief, and forget about fading Time.

What are 'living water' and 'the garden of paradise'
but to savor rare wine by the shore of the river.

The upright man and the crazy drunk come from a common stock—
whose path will seduce us, which shall we choose?

What does the quiet sky know of secrets behind the veil?
O big-shot Inquisitor, why fight with the one who holds the veil?

If our reckless sins were always considered…
what about the grace and mercy of the one who nourishes all?

The pious wants a drink from the clear spring of water, Hafiz wants
only wine; I wonder which he'll satisfy, the One who accomplishes all.

Love's Order

Have you heard the teaching of the harp and lute?
'Drink wine in secret, the police say it's apostasy.'

'Forget love's riddle, that seductive wink...'
It's painful to hear their words.

They ignore love's order and the grace of those in love,
they repel the youth and offend the elder.

Outside the door, deceived by shadows...
What's happening behind the veil?

They bring their petty squabbles to the sage...
what disciples! always harassing the master.

A hundred honors purchased with a single wink
but even the fairest lovers can't negotiate the deal.

Some think union with the Friend is the fruit of work and struggle,
others surrender everything and trust the divine decree.

In the end, there's no sure foothold in the field of time—
it's like a tailor-shop, constant exchange and alteration.

Get drunk! everyone—the saint, Hafiz, preacher and religious police—
if you look too close, we're all a bit hypocritical.

Wasted

Your braid of hair bound a thousand hearts on a single strand
and cut off from all directions those who would set us free.

That lovers might waste their souls on the fragrant breeze
he opened his pouch of incense and sealed the door of yearning.

Restless and discontent…like the new moon, my beloved shows forth
the slim crescent of her eyebrow, then her full radiant face—then vanishes.

The bringer of wine splashed every-colored drink in our golden cups—
on the curved walls of the chalice, what marvelous pictures!

Ah, what music, as the blood of the wine-cask poured into our morning cup,
what gurgling delicious murmurs as it coursed through the slender bottle-neck.

In that session beyond the screen, what note did the singer hit
that closed off the noise of the world and opened the way to mystery?

Hafiz, those who long for union but refuse to work
are like unclean pilgrims circling the shrine.

A Gamble

Strike up a song, one that can strike my ravaged heart,
knock out a poem as I knock back wine.

Lay your head on the doorstep of the fair one
and you will sing out boldly as the nightingale, holding up your head.

The curve of my stooped figure may seem to be useless
but it's a bow whose arrow can yet strike my enemy's face.

The mysterious play of love is missing from public worship.
The cup of wisdom must be drunk among the wise.

No wandering dervish owns the goods of a sultan;
we have only our tattered robes, not worth tossing on the fire.

Those who see bet everything, both worlds for a single vision.
At the very first throw of the dice true lovers risk all they are.

Should fortune open the gate to his inmost court
we could lay our weary heads, dreaming, on his doorstep.

All I want is love, youth, and drunken wandering—
so when the mysteries pile up I can serve as interpreter.

It's no surprise: your braid has become a highway robber
sure to strike a hundred caravans.

Hafiz, in the power of the word, renounce all pretence and hypocrisy.
Perhaps, in this fading world, a word of hope may still be said.

Foundations

Haunting my time at prayer: the curve of your eyebrow
like the arch in this quiet prayer-niche… My concentration's gone.

From now on, don't expect me to be patient and sensible,
all that forbearance and character's been thrown to the wind.

The wine has grown pure, and the birds in the orchard completely drunk,
the season for lovers, the time of the serious work at last begun.

From its deepest roots the reeking world grew fragrant.
The rose brought joy, and the morning breeze supreme delight.

O Bride of Artistry, do not brood over your sorry fate,
adorn the room of beauty, for the bridegroom comes.

Those saccharine frauds got all dressed up…
but the Stealer of Hearts arrived with true and gracious beauty.

Trees too rooted to the ground are all weighed down.
O happy cypress, who spread your strong branches without regret.

Singer! belt out the words of Hafiz in a roaring drunken ghazal
until I cry with complete abandon, remembering my joy.

A Share in the Cup

How can a shattered heart speak eloquent poems?
one subtle verse from your book and all our words grew luminous.

Should I gain, from the jewel of your face, a signet ring and power
I would place all the kingdoms of Solomon beneath its precious stone.

O heart, don't fret about the insults of the envious,
look deeper and you may find good in this as well.

If my poems don't thrill the reader—whoever he is,
however brilliant—surely his own work is counterfeit.

In the circle of fate, all have been given
a share in the cup, the life-blood of true desire.

As to the grape and wine, it's been written from before the dawn:
some are meant for the market, others for behind the veil.

God forbid that Hafiz should forget his drunken friends,
it's been written from before the dawn: he will remember them.

Horizon

Over the years, I've sold my books in exchange for wine,
my prayer and doctrine spent on the adornment of the tavern.

Behold, the true devotion of the Magian sage: in his eyes,
generous, serene, whatever we drunkards did was beautiful.

Drench all our scholarship with finest wine
for I have seen the Horizon— and he scoffed at my learned pose.

'O heart, if you want to see virtuous beauty, behold the idols'—
the words of one versed in the science of the gaze.

The compass of the heart revolved in all directions,
in dizzy wandering circles it spun without stop.

Drunk with bliss, the vocalist began to sing
and the stiff-necked scholars in the crowd wept blood.

I blossomed like a streamside rose
in the shade of the noble cypress.

The master forbade slandering the Sufis in their sky-blue robes
so the legends of their miracles might thrive and spread.

In the master's presence, Hafiz won't pay out his gilded coins—
that merchant would catch out counterfeit at once.

The Counterfeiter

With the chalice of rare wine held now in the petals of the rose
the nightingale cries in a thousand tongues.

Look for the right book of poems and take the desert road alone.
Who's got time for seminary, commentators on comments?

Go alone, like the eagle to its cliff-side perch,
the cry of the beggar echoing from peak to peak.

Last night, drunk himself, the dean of the seminary ordered:
'No more wine—though it's better than a huge inheritance.'

Last dregs or finest vintage, the law can't say. Drink up!
The bringer of the true wine bears the origin of blessing.

Forget second-rate attorneys, their jargon and bar-room gossip.
Sure, he can weave, but you don't put the plaiter of mats in a silk-shop.

Careful Hafiz, watch over these words like chunks of gold,
the city counterfeiter runs the national bank.

Servant of the Cup

Come friend, the cup is a shining mirror,
behold the clear wine, its crimson hue like a ruby.

Seek the secret behind the veil from the wandering dervish drunks
for preening pseudo-sufis are barred from the inner room.

Put away your snares, the dove cannot be caught.
In this life traps catch nothing but wind.

Strive, but free of care. When the waters of blessing ran dry
Adam had to leave the garden, the dwelling of health and wholeness.

When the cup is passed around, take a drink or two and
carry on—that is, don't expect lasting union.

You are old, heart, and have yet to harvest one rose from leisure—
at least let your grey hair help you in cultivating honor.

On the porch of your dwelling we have praised you faithfully.
Master, look upon your slave once more in mercy.

Hafiz has become an adept of the wine-cup. Dawn breeze, go
to that Master and send him the service of his favorite slave.

Jasmine

A full cup of wine in hand, the beloved in my heart's desire…
On a day like this, the Sultan of the World is my fawning slave.

Tonight, no need to bring candles to our gathering—
the face of the Friend will be, among us, our full resplendent moon.

Forget the rest—in my book, wine is legal—but
without your face, noble cypress, slender rose, wine is criminal.

Please—no store-bought perfume at our gatherings, however sweet.
At each eye-blink the air is soaked by the fragrant hair of the beloved.

My ear is forever on the word of the reed-flute, the murmuring harp—
my eye on the wine-red lips, the cup passed around among revelers.

Forget sugar, and the most exquisite candy—
all I want is the taste of your lips on mine.

Ever since this keening need for you has gripped my heart
the dark back corner of the tavern's been my only place of refuge.

Of honor and shame, why say more? My good name is ruined.
You ask me who I am? A clue: infamy's my middle name.

I may be a sodden drunk, with mixed up thoughts and leering eyes…
but, in *this* city, not one of you is any better.

Go ahead—lodge a complaint with the Chief Prohibitionist,
he's as greedy for a drink as I am.

Hafiz, don't go for long without a glass of wine, and Love,
for the time of fasting is over and the days of jasmine come.

Overdose

As long as wine can be named, and there's a sign out front of the tavern,
our heads will be trampled dust on the master's path.

From before eternity I have worn the gold ring of the master:
Ever we are as we are, and ever shall it be.

Should you pass over my grave, say a prayer in hope
it will be a place of pilgrimage for drunks and all the wretched.

Get lost you preening ascetic! neither one of us can
see through the veil, and neither one of us ever will.

Ravisher of every heart, my beloved has strolled off drunk,
capturing the gaze of all, overthrowing nations.

I long for you: from the night my poor eye slumps to its grave
            overdosed on gazing at your beauty
until the morning when all shall rise…

Hafiz—if your luck doesn't get any better, someone else
may be running their hand through the hair of your beloved.

The Drug

Last night, in fragrant words, the violet spoke to the rose:
The tress of a certain You-Know-Who brought affliction into this world.

When my heart had become a storehouse of mysteries, Providence
locked the door and left the key with the beloved.

I came to you with a shattered heart. The doctor
wrote me a prescription for the drug of your gracious beauty.

He scoffed when he saw me on the street, a wretched beggar:
See what my lover has made of himself. What can he offer?

May his body be filled with health and strength, his spirit with delight—
he came near when I was helpless, stretching out his hand.

Counselor, follow your own advice,
wine and the beautiful aren't hurting anyone.

Drunk or Sober

You want me to give up drinking? What a stupid idea.
I have at least enough reason to reject such nonsense.

After beating the drum and strumming the harp on the path of wisdom
should I go back to dried-up piety? No thanks.

Go easy on those who abstain from wine,
no one reaches love without the benefit of guidance.

I've become the slave of the one who released me from ignorance,
everything he does reveals the face of true communion.

I didn't know where the path to the tavern would lead,
if I had I would have tossed my baggage sooner.

The stuck-up abstinent and pious or the wine-drunk poor one,
which of these enjoys your favor?

I couldn't sleep last night, worried by the words of the preacher:
If Hafiz gets drunk, there's going to be trouble.

The Clay Chalice

Last night I saw the messengers knock on the wine-house door.
They molded our mortal clay into a noble chalice.

Sublime dwellers from beyond the celestial veil
they sat with me drunk at the roadside, and passed a bottle.

Not even the sky took on the burden; only man,
distraught now, wretched, dared to attempt the work of faith.

A chaos of denominations means innumerable loopholes.
When they did not see truth, they set out on the route of fables.

When peace reigned between us at last, the celestial virgins
danced, and raised high the cup of Thanksgiving.

Never mind the wavering candle-flame, the true fire's known
by the ash heap of smoldering moths at its base.

No one has unveiled the true face of thought like Hafiz,
the tress of each verse: combed and curled to perfection.

Sugar

May your flesh be kept from all affliction, the doctor far off,
and your inner self protected from every wound.

What more is the happiness of all the world than the radiance of your
own pure happiness? May nothing ever block your path.

When autumn seeps in, plundering the orchard,
may it not find a path to the noble cypress.

The earth, unfurled like a woven rug, radiates your glory—
may those who would defile its grace be stifled.

Outer shell and inner kernel depend upon your happiness—
may your flesh be kept from illness and your spirit free of care.

Anyone casting an evil glance on the moonlike beauty of your face…
may their eyes become like worthless seeds cast into the fire.

Seek healing in the words of Hafiz— they rain down sugar in torrents—
and forget about second-rate candy.

Transformations

A lone star like a flash of lightning, became the moon of our anxious heart,
the friend, the soul-mate of the whole congregation.

My love, who never set foot in the dim scriptorium or wrote a line of her own
became, in her pleading glance, Instructor of all the learned.

His fragrance borne on the morning breeze, the sick heart of lovers became
ransom for the cheek of the wild rose, the eye of the narcissus.

At the tavern, the Friend has given me a seat of honor,
Behold! the least beggar in the city, high priest of the congregation.

Delight brims over from the court of Love
for the arched eyebrow of the Friend now takes over as architect.

For God's sake: let me purify my lips with a drop of wine,
parched by sin, my heart began to murmur temptations.

Your sly, enchanting wink, doled out wine for the mystics
that tranquilized Knowledge, and left Reason numb.

Turn away your reins from the path to the tavern
for Hafiz went down that road and wound up wrecked.

If the rough copper of my words turned to the glistering gold of existence,
the patronage of wealthy friends has worked the transformation.

Headless

The one rapt in yearning for the unseen face of the friend,
surely he will reap the harvest of his vision.

Like the tip of his pen our heads are bent in obedience
to the word of his command (perhaps for decapitation)!

Like a burnt wax candle, its wick cut over and over
your lover keeps putting his head on the block.

He laid his head so often on your porch he became
its doorstep; in reward he was able to kiss your feet.

I'm sick of this dried up piety—bring the true wine!
a mere hint of its bouquet can refresh my heart.

If you get nothing else out of wine, at least it gives you
a break from the seductive whisperings of reason.

Having never set foot beyond the doorstep of piety
now he wants to travel on the road to the tavern!

Hafiz will go to the grave with a shattered heart—
like the black mark in the tulip, his unmet longing.

'The Mirror of Princes'

My heart has no other path than the friendship of those I love—
whatever alternate routes I devise, it refuses.

For God's sake, stop prattling on, and tell me about the beloved!
there's no more exquisite thought than the image of her face.

Hidden behind my books I guzzle the purest wine,
amazed that my burning hypocrisy has not yet scorched the page.

Soon I will throw my coat-of-many-colors on the fire
for the master won't take it in exchange for wine.

Surely, in the gathering of friends, the ruby wine is pure—
its jewel holds only the absolute.

The one preaching at the drunks defies the will of Providence.
I think his heart is narrow and he needs a drink himself.

Although dismayed, I have to laugh—I'm like a blazing candle
at the gathering, but some just won't catch fire.

Soon, like Alexander, I will shine in the mirror of princes
whether my fire spreads or not.

It's exquisite, how you've tracked my heart down; I boast of your seductive glance—
never has a wild bird been snared with such elegance.

Surely we are poor, and the Beloved alone has boundless wealth—
what good is there trying to seduce the only true Stealer of Hearts?

For God's sake, mercy! the dervish at the gate to your street
has no other path—and wouldn't take it if he did.

I wouldn't be surprised if, for such fresh and eloquent poems,
the Emperor should clothe poor Hafiz head to foot in gold.

At the Foot of the Wine-cask

Before the Friend, rhetorical display is tactless—
the tongue is hushed, but the mouth is soaked with Arabic.

Between the meek angelic glance and the demon's seductive wink,
reason is reduced to ash, and the mind astonished.

Don't bother asking why the earth is so generous to hypocrites;
there's no reason for its lavish charity.

In the orchard of this world, no one plucks a thorn-less rose.
With the prophet's lamp comes the torch of the enemy.

I wouldn't spend half a cent for the courtyard of these pseudo-sufis.
I have set up camp on the tavern's couch, at the foot of the wine-cask.

It's the gorgeous daughter of the grape that brightens my glance.
Perhaps we see the world through the veil of purple in the glass.

Seek the remedy for grief in that refreshing drink
that cheers both the wine-glass of China and the Syrian cup.

Bring me wine; worn out by constant begging like Hafiz
I weep in the morning and pray through the night.

A Game of Glances

When the image of your face reflected off the surface of the cup
the sage, filled with such delicious wine, was seized with furious craving.

From beneath the veil, on the day of Alast, the rays of your glorious face
fell among illusions and specters.

In all these images of wine, the whole array of shadows
it is one ray of light from the face of Love that fell upon the wine-cup.

Jealous of what they know, his lovers keep silence.
How then have the many heard of this mystery of yearning?

It's not my fault I fell from the mosque to the tavern,
this path was marked out for me from the Day of Alast.

What can be done when, locked in circles like a compass, you can't move on?
Such is everyone trapped in the cycle of days.

Struck by the scimitar of fierce desire, keep on dancing—
to be slain by Love is a blissful destiny.

Over the well of your dimpled chin I clung to the curl of your tress…
out of the pit, into a noose!

Master, never again will I stray outside—
I belong in the radiance of his face, on the lip of the wine-cup.

With every breath, new grace floods into my ravished heart.
Behold this destitute beggar: laden with gifts!

Though Sufis compete in a game of seductive glances,
Hafiz, with his ravished heart, has the worst reputation of them all.

Hooked

When the friend took the cup in hand
the idols in the square were shattered.

I have fallen at his feet, grieving—
will he ever take hold of my hand?

Dropped in the sea like a fish—
until the Friend with his hook should raise me up.

Whoever has caught his glance will ask:
What policeman could arrest the drunkard?

His heart will bloom within him, who, like Hafiz,
has drawn a cup of wine from the day of Alast.

On the Shore

In the sweatshop of Time and Space the end-product amounts to: nothing.
Bring more wine—for the ways and means of the world mean nothing.

The desire for a free communion of friends comes from deep in the heart—
a true desire—were it not, heart and soul would amount to nothing.

Forget the blessings of the sidra, the shade of the Tree of Paradise,
when you arrive, my fragrant cypress, these others seem less than nothing.

Without struggle or sacrifice, the gift falls into your lap,
otherwise: not even the fruit of Love's garden can help.

For less than a week you have rested in this roadside tavern—
enjoy the break in your pilgrimage, for all of Time leads to nothing.

Bringer of wine, on the lip, on the shore of annihilation, come to us
once more; for the space between lip and mouth is less than nothing.

Consumed with grief, my days are spent in groaning and constant tears.
To me, propriety and explanations mean nothing.

Strict ascetic, be careful not to boast of your superior traditions,
the road from the cloister to the Magian shrine is almost nothing.

Though the name of Hafiz has come to be praised throughout the world,
to the holy renegade honor and shame mean nothing.

Thrown

I wept a flood, tossed patience onto the desert floor.
Absorbed in such work, I threw my heart into the sea.

From the tense, constricted heart of sin, I heave a sigh
casting flame upon the sin of Eve and Adam.

Shot through with arrows by the Light…Give me wine:
drunk, I'll sling a noose around the neck of its quiver.

Sprinkling wine on the seat of honor
I strum my lute toward the sky-blue dome.

The root of happiness remains with the keeper of hearts.
I work hard to throw myself before him.

Sun-lit moon, remove the cord of your veil, that like your hair,
let down to the ground, I may throw my poor head at your feet.

O Hafiz: if it's foolish to rest on passing time
why leave the pleasure of today for tomorrow?

The Flood

The nightingale drank from the source of envy and gained in reward the rose
but the jealous wind torments him with a hundred thorns.

The parrot dreamed of sugar and his imaginings made him glad
when a flash-flood of nothingness erased his thoughts.

Let thoughts of him, the heart's ripe fruit, refresh my thirsty gaze
though he vanished without a trace and left my work in ruins.

Driver, I've lost my load—for God's sake, help!
hope alone has made me a traveler in this caravan.

Don't laugh at my dust-worn face and streaming eyes—
enfolding us in joy, the sky itself is made from these elements.

Weep and lament, the foreign moon of envy
made my own moon, the bow of his eyebrow, to hide in the grave.

I could have taken the king-side rook, but missed the chance.
What can I do? the swift play of time made me careless.

Shipwrecked

For God's sake, help! I'm losing control of my heart—
if all of this gets out…what a disaster!

We're shipwrecked—fair wind, come,
send us home! that we may see the Friend once more.

At first the world seems charming and safe like a bed-time story…
Count life the occasion for mercy and gentleness.

In the circle of friends, the home of the rose, and wine, the plaintive song
of the nightingale: Bring the dawn wine— O drunks, fly to the Beloved!

Behold the shining wine-cup, Alexander's mirror
and you will see things as they are in the kingdom of Darius.

Loving friend, grateful for your astounding gifts
seek out that wandering dervish stripped of everything but love for you.

To live free of care in this world and the next:
be generous with friends and respect your enemies.

It was fate that kept us from a good reputation;
if you don't like our ways, go ahead, try fighting with destiny itself!

The 'daughter of the grape' whom the squeamish call 'mother of evil'…
more delicious than the kiss of maidens.

In this stingy world, stay free of care, delight in wine
the drink that made a beggar into Qarun.

Bringer of wine, tell the good news to the elders:
the eloquent Persian poets have come to give us life!

O grand ascetic in your spotless gown,
don't blame Hafiz for his wine-soaked robe!

The Arc

There's no way to lay hold of your tress,
to rest on your fickle promise…or the morning breeze.

I struggled hard to seek your face
but there's no changing the divine decree.

I shed my blood to grasp the hem of his robe…
Don't let go! even when the orthodox mock you.

There's no way to liken his face to the moon on the dark horizon,
no family resemblance to anything vain.

When my towering Cypress arrives for the hymns
I tear apart my robe in bliss.

The subtlety of love is beyond all thought
and cannot be unraveled by earthly minds.

What can I say? you're so good and gracious, when I pray
I can't keep quiet, but shout out loud for joy.

Only the clear gaze sees the face of the beloved,
only the pure can peer into this mirror.

I grew jealous—for all the world's your lover—
but one can't fight against the whole creation.

To the heart of Hafiz, your eyebrow is the arc of his prayer-niche—
for us, obedience is given to you alone.

The Pearl

The monk in his cell—what does he care about the scenery?
On the street of the Friend, who needs a dried up wasteland?

Beloved soul, by your very need for God alone
spare one breath to ask about *our* need.

Gorgeous sovereign—for God's sake, I'm burnt to a crisp!
please, look into it, learn about our need for you.

We're the very sovereigns of neediness, too poor to ask for anything…
but then, in the presence of the Friend, who needs to ask?

Bent on capturing souls, you have no need of prologues…
When everything is yours, what need is there to plunder?

The enlightening mind of the Friend: a world-reflecting wine-cup—
why show forth our need where everything is known?

My days of adventure at sea have passed—
with the pearl in hand, why bother sailing?

Poor wretch, the life-giving lips of the Friend
know the full depth of your need—why keep begging?

Orthodox police, get lost! there's nothing between us—
the friends have come together…who needs enemies?

Enough talk Hafiz, the gift shines forth by itself—
why bother fighting the accuser?

Notes

The source for all translations is Parvīz Nātal Khānlarī's critical edition of Hafiz – *Diwān-e Hāfiz* (Tehran 1983). In the notes which follow, each of our English poems is referenced by its original *ghazal* number, followed by the initial Persian line as found in Khānlarī's *Diwān*. Numbers in parentheses then indicate lines within our translations.

Escape-Route

(*Diwān*, 367: بیا تا گل بر افشانیم و می در ساغر اندازیم)

(4) all of us: lit. من و ساقی (I and *Sāqī*); the poet and the mythical dispenser of wine.

(9) courtyard of the Beautiful: lit. عالی جناب (high threshold).

(11) grace and charm: lit. طامات (vainglory, incoherent statements).

(14) cup: lit. خمت (jar, vat); clear pool of Paradise: حوض کوثر (the pool of *Kawthar*), a reference to the eponymous, celestial river of the Qur'ān's 108th chapter.

The Dregs

(*Diwān*, 22: زلف آشفته و خوی کرده و خندان لب و مست)

The gender of the Persian third-person pronoun (او) and possessive enclitic (اش) is indefinite, allowing for an ambiguity of gender within Hafiz' originals; throughout *The Tangled Braid*, we alternate between he, she and He in translating this gender ambiguity.

(3-4) bold...petulant: lit. lip expressing sorrow, derision (افسوس); bed: lit. بالین (pillow).

(9-10) teetotalling wretch: lit. زاهد (ascetic); Alast, i.e. آلست (Am I not?), a reference to the primordial covenant established when God demanded of His creatures Am I not your Lord? (*Alastu birabbikum?*; see the Qur'ān 7:172).

(12) wine of love: lit. باده مست (wine of intoxication).

The Courier

(*Diwān*, 467: نسیم صبح سعادت بدان نشان که تو دانی)

(2) You-Know-Who: lit. فلان, an Arabic substitute for a proper name, i.e. Mr. So-and-So.

(3) secret: lit. mystery of the *khalvat* (خلوت), the Sufi chamber of spiritual seclusion.

(8) love: lit. روی کرامت ([in] a generous way).

(9) lit. The idea of your sword to us is the traditional saying of the thirsty-one and water.

(12) The meaning's not so obvious: lit. در آن میان...دقیقه ایست (there's a subtlety...in that middle).

Bankrupt
(مطلب طاعت و پیمان و صلاح از من مست :Diwān, 21)
(1) safe: lit. طاعت (obedience, pious deed).
(4) blessings: i.e. تکبیر (takbīr), the act of declaring *Allāhu akbar* (God is greater/greatest).
(5) fortune: lit. سر قضا (mystery of destiny).
(7-8) span...ant: lit. The mountain waist is smaller than the ant waist; stop knocking...grace: lit. do not be unhopeful of the door of mercy (در رحمت).
(9) rapt...reflection: lit. نرگس مستانه (intoxicated narcissus [eye]).
(14) nothing: lit. از وصل تواش نیست (nothing of union [with] you).

Worthless
(گل بی رخ یار خوش نباشد :Diwān, 159)
(4) light of your face: lit. لاله عذار (tulip of cheek).
(6) your voice: lit. صوت هزار (voice of nightingale or voice of a thousand).
(7) everything you say: lit. شکر لب (sugar lip [of the beloved]).
(11) lit. Every picture fixed by the hand of reason (دست عقل).

The Box of Jewels
(اگر روم ز پیاش فتنهها برانگیزد :Diwān, 151)
(3) lit. If, in road-traversing, for one moment, from desire

Accounting
(مزن بر دل ز نوك غمزه تیرم :Diwān, 324)
(2) piercing: lit. بیمار (ill, afflicting eye of the beloved).
(4) surplus: lit. زكات (zakāt), alms-giving prescribed within Islam.
(12) Master: lit. پیر مغان (Master of the Magians), the authentic esoteric guide.
(13-14) fraud: lit. زاهد (ascetic); fruit of the tree: lit. سیب بوستان (orchard apple).

Stairway to the Sun
(دوش از جناب آصف پیك بشارت آمد :Diwān, 167)
(1-2) messenger...King: lit. آصف (Asif) and سلیمان (Sulaimān), legendary vice-regent and scriptural king within Islamic traditions.
(3) mingled with: lit. گل کن (make into clay).

(5) Countless…books: lit. گفتند...این شرح بی نهایت (They spoke this endless explanation).

(9) each of us: lit. هر کس...ز خوبان (every one of the beautiful).

(11) throne: lit. تخت جم (throne of *Jam*), the celebrated, mythological Persian king.

Five Days of Freedom
(دل سراپرده محبت اوست :*Diwān*, 60)

(3) this world or the next: lit. دو کون (two worlds).

Secrets of the Empty Cell
(حسنت به اتفاق ملاحت جهان گرفت :*Diwān*, 87)

(4) the secret: lit. سر دلش (his heart's secret).

(12) face of the Beautiful: lit. عارض ساقی (cheek of the *Sāqī*).

(20) sorrow…lute: lit. از غم کران گرفت (from grief [the Sufi] took up the lute).

(21-22) life: lit. لطف (grace); the envious: حاسد (*hāsid*), a term suggestive of the Devil (see the Qur'ān 113:5).

Bound
(خدا چو صورت ابروی دلگشای تو بست :*Diwān*, 33)

(2) me: lit. کار من (my work).

(10) bound: lit. عهد...بست (established covenant [with]).

(11) paradise: lit. حیات دگر (another life).

Overnight Delivery
(برید باد صبا دوشم آگهی آورد :*Diwān*, 143)

(4) robe: lit. جامه (garment), but also suggestive more specifically of a Sufi gown.

(5) Friend watching over us: lit. عنایت دوست (the Friend's solicitude).

(7-8) you: lit. حور (*hūr*), i.e. celestial virgin (see the Qur'ān 55:72); doorman of paradise: lit. *Rizvān* (رضوان), legendary figure who guards the entrance to heaven.

(10) cloth cap: lit. کلاه, a conic hat or turban worn by Sufis.

(11) radiant face: lit. عارض آن ماه خرگهی (cheek of that tabernacled moon).

(13) Victor: lit. *Mansūr* (منصور), Shah of Persia.

The King's Highway
(به سر جام جم آنگه نظر توانی کرد :*Diwān*, 137)

(1) the King: lit. جم ([king] *Jam*).

(9-10) drug of his presence: lit. چاره ذوق حضور (remedy of the taste of the presence); those who know: lit. اهل نظر (folk of vision).

(17) the light: lit. نور ریاضت (light of [spiritual] exercise).

Caravans
(ای هدهد صبا به سبا می‌فرستمت :Diwān, 91)

(1-2) Noble crowned bird: i.e. هدهد (hoopoe), the intermediary between Solomon and the Queen of Sheba.

(4) your original home: lit. آسمان وفا (the heavens of fidelity).

(12) peace: lit. دوا (remedy).

(13) close to your lovers: lit. همنشین دل (the heart's fellow-sitter).

(15) love: lit. تفرج (recreation, delight in viewing).

The Compass
(در نظربازی ما بیخبران حیرانند :Diwān, 188)

(8) robe: lit. خرقه پشمین, the woollen *khirqah* worn by Sufis.

(10) hypocrites: lit. عشقبازان (love-players).

(16) true sober intoxication: lit. مستوری و مستی (temperance and intoxication).

(17) young seekers: lit. مغبچگان (young Magians).

(19-20) paradise: lit. نزهتگه ارواح (pleasure place of spirits); it: lit. عقل و جان (reason and soul).

(21) saint: lit. زاهد (ascetic)

(22) memorize the scripture: lit. قرآن خوانند (recite the Qur'ān).

A Night of Candles
(مدامم مست می‌دارد نسیم جعد گیسویت :Diwān, 94)

(4) curved...eyebrow: lit. محراب, the *mihrāb* or arched niche indicating direction of prayer.

(5-6) retinas: lit. سواد لوح بینش (black tablet of vision); the library of the Beautiful: lit. نقش خال هندویت (image of your black mole).

(9) fawning prayers: lit. رسم فنا (custom of annihilation).

(13) end of time: lit. ز دنیی و از عقبی (from the world and the afterlife).

The Jeweler
(یاد باد آنکه نهانت نظری با ما بود :Diwān, 200)

(4) the free gift of Jesus: lit. معرج عیسویت (the Jesus-like miracle).

(10) over...wine: lit. صهبا بود (was the red wine).

(13) the Friend: lit. مه من (my moon).

(17-18) renderings: lit. اصلاح شما (your [pl.] correcting); the solid pearls of Hafiz: Persian lines are often portrayed as pearls strung together to produce composite poems.

The Work
(چو باد عزم سر کوی یار خواهم کرد :131 ,*Diwān*)
  (2) soaked: lit. مشكبار (laden with musk); her braided hair: lit. خوشش
      (her beauty).
  (9) lit. As my dawn candle became enlightened by his *mihr* [i.e. sun
      or love].
  (14) path: طریق (*tarīq*), way, road, suggestive more specifically of the
       Sufi path.

On the Road to Aiman
(ای نسیم سحر آرامگه یار کجاست :27 ,*Diwān*)
  (1-2) beloved: lit. آرامگه یار (friend's resting place); where has she gone:
        lit. منزل...کجاست (where is…the abode).
  (3-4) valley of Aiman: the right side of the valley from which Moses
        was first called by God, before his vision of the miraculous burning
        on Mt. Sinai; see the Qur'ān 28:29-30.
  (9-10) masterwork: lit. هزاران کار (thousands[-fold] work); who would
         dare reproach us: lit.ملامتگر بیکار کجاست (where is the work-less
         blamer?).
  (13) Wine-bringer…wine: a textual variant within the critical edition,
       alternate for the primary reading of Wine, minstrel and rose
       (باده و مطرب و گل).

The Tangled Braid
(جمالش آفتاب هر نظر باد :100 ,*Diwān*)
  (2) fleeting charms: lit. خوبی (beauty, goodness)
  (3) bird of paradise: هما (*humā*), fabulous eagle or phoenix; a prophetic
      symbol.
  (8) poison of envy: lit. خون جگر (blood of the liver).

On the Way
(راهیست راه عشق که هیچش کناره نیست :73 ,*Diwān*)
  (4) approval: lit. استخاره, i.e. seeking divine favor, augury.
  (8) counties of the heart: lit. ولایت ما (our dominion, district).

Lack
(روشنی طلعت تو ماه ندارد :123 ,*Diwān*)
  (8) care-free: lit. خانقاه ندارد ([who] does not have a Sufi lodge).
  (11) hide your wound: lit. خون خور (drink blood).

The Tangled Braid

(13) stark black: lit. تطاول (tyranny, insolence).

(18) well of jealousy: lit. خون جگر (blood of the liver).

Surrender

(الا يا ايها الساقى ادر كاسا و ناولها :Diwān, 1)

(4) fragrance: lit. بوی نافهای (musk-pod scent).

(13) if…near: lit. حضوری گر همی خواهی (if you desire presence).

Stung

(گر می فروش حاجت رندان روا کند :Diwān, 181)

(9) Seeker: lit. حکیم (physician, philosopher, learned one).

(12) needless work: lit. فضولی (busy-body, prattling).

Snared

(به دام زلف تو دل مبتلای خویشتن است :Diwān, 51)

(5) exotic perfumes: lit. مشك چین و چگل (the musk of *Chīn* and *Chigil*), i.e. China and a city in Turkistan, both renowned for their perfumes.

(7-8) beloved: lit. بت شیرین (sweet idol); burn…up: lit. فنای ([mystic] annihilation).

(12) your soul: lit. عافیتت (your welfare, prosperity).

Scorched

(ای غایب از نظر به خدا می‌سپارمت :Diwān, 92)

(6) hand: lit. دست دعا (hand of prayer).

(7) the gods of Babylon: lit. هاروت (*Hārūt*), one of the two angels who tested the Babylonian peoples with magic (Qur'ān 2:102).

(13) drunken erotic escapades: lit. شراب و شاهد و رندی (wine, beloved and drunkenness).

Loss in Translation

(نه هر که چهره بر افروخت دلبری داند :Diwān, 174)

(2) princes can mirror Alexander; Hafiz makes several references to Alexander (سکندر), evoking a popular tradition which associates this conqueror with The Mirror of Princes, a text purportedly written for Alexander by Aristotle as an instruction manual for emperors.

Cracked

(دوش در حلقه ما قصه گیسوی تو بود :Diwān, 204)

(8) panic: lit. فتنه (discord, tribulation).

(9) the upright: lit. اهل سلامت (people of security, probity).

Daydreams

(برو به کار خود ای واعظ این چه فریادست :Diwān, 36)

(1) Stupid accuser: lit. واعظ (admonisher), Hafiz' orthodox opponent.

(5) One: lit. خدا (God).

(7) universe: lit. هشت خلد (eight paradise[s]).

(10) ruined metropolis: i.e. خراب آباد; the ruins of love are the poet's only foundations.

(14) lit. کزین فسانه و افسون مرا بسی یادست (For I have in memory many of these tales and spells).

Bloodshot

(شاهدان گر دلبری زین سان کنند :Diwān, 192)

(2) orthodox: lit. زاهدان (ascetics).

(4) his lovers: lit. گلرخانش (his rose-cheeked ones).

(5-6) Virtuoso: lit. یار ما (our friend); holy ones: lit. قدسیان بر عرش (holy ones before the celestial throne).

(7-8) the addressee is here likened to both a player and a piece of equipment within the game of *chaugān* (i.e. polo).

(12) injustice and grief: lit. ظلم بر انسان (injustice to mankind).

(14) Noah's flood: lit. آن حکایتها که از طوفان (these stores which concern the deluge).

(17) the wise: lit. اهل راز (the folk of mystery).

Sacked and Plundered

(صبا وقت سحر بوئی ز زلف یار می‌آورد :Diwān, 142)

(3) form like a fir-tree: lit. شکل صنوبر (figure of a fir-tree).

(6) no escape...ravaged: lit. بدان هنجار ([followed] on that road).

(7) lit. From the roof of his palace, I saw the light of the moon shining.

(9) lit. At the word of minstrel and *Sāqī*, I went out at all times.

(16) yearning heart: lit. سر بیمار (sick head).

The Secret of the Work

(گفتم غم تو دارم گفتا غمت سرآید :Diwān, 227)

The lines of this dialogical ghazal alternate between گفتم and گفتا (I said; he/she said).

(4) can't...work: lit. این کار کمتر آید (this work little comes).

A Drop of Rain

(حافظ خلوت نشین دوش به میخانه شد :Diwān, 165)

The Tangled Braid

(1) lonely hermit: lit. خلوت نشین (cloister-sitting).

(5) monk: lit. صوفی (Sufi).

(7) young novice: lit. مغبچهای...راهزن دین و دل (Magian youth...highway-man of religion and heart).

(14) lit. Our circle of superogatory prayers became a sitting-circle of fables.

The Orchard of Delight
(روضه خلد برین خلوت درویشان است :Diwān, 50)

This ghazal's recurrent line-final phrase (*radīf*) is درویشان است (is... [of] dervishes), which we render variously throughout this English translation.

(2) lit. مایه محتشمی خدمت درویشان است (The source of power is the service of dervishes).

(3) gold-hoard of loneliness (گنج عزلت), a textual variant within the critical edition, alternate for گنج عزت (treasure of glory).

(5) castle...side: lit. قصر فردوس (palace of paradise); bearing...whirls: lit. منظری (scene, spectacle).

(10) courtesy: lit. حمشت (pomp).

(12) triumph: lit. فرصت (leisure, advantage).

(15) Qarun: i.e. قارون, the biblical Korah, known in the Qur'ān for his avarice (28:76).

(17) politician: lit. توانگر (powerful one).

(23-24) This stanza is a textual variant within the critical edition, which includes a different *takhallus* (i.e. the line featuring Hafiz' signature) as its penultimate stanza.

The Sultan's Crown
(دمی با غم بسر بردن جهان یکسر نمیارزد :Diwān, 147)

(9) flood: i.e. طوفان; recalling the Qur'ānic account of Noah's flood (29:14).

(12) captives: lit. لشگر (army).

Glitter
(این پیک نامور که رسید از دیار دوست :Diwān, 62)

(3) strength and beauty: lit. جمال و جلال (beauty and glory); two attributes of God.

(11-12) End Times: lit. فتنه (discord, tribulation); me: lit. ما و چراغ چشم (us and the lamp of the eye).

(13) glitter to mix with mascara: lit. کحل الجواهری (collyrium blended with ground pearls).

Every Morning, Wind

(دوش آگهی ز یار سفر کرده داد باد :98 ,*Diwān*)

(1) has arrived: lit. سفر کرده (made [a] journey).

(5) defenceless: lit. بی حفاظ (*bī hifāz*, without protection), recalling Hafiz' own name.

A Handful of Sand

(هر انکه جانب اهل وفا نگه دارد :118 ,*Diwān*)

(4) keep…bargain: lit. keep guard over the end of the rope (رشته; c.f. the Qur'ān 3:103).

(8) heart…love: lit. حق صحبت و عهد وفا (the right of fellowship and covenant of fidelity).

(14) he'll take care of me: lit. خدا نگه دارد ([may] God have care).

The Book of Delight

(در ازل پرتو حسنت ز تجلی دم زد :148 ,*Diwān*)

(1-6) These verses recall the Qur'ān's account of the creation of Adam, and Satan's subsequent rebellious jealousy (see, for example, the Qur'ān 20:116 and ff.).

(4) us: lit. آدم (Adam).

(6) wars…hatred: lit. برهم (confusion).

(7-8) court of Beauty: lit. تماشاگه راز (theatre of mystery).

Plunder

(درخت دوستی بنشان که کام دل به بار آرد :111 ,*Diwān*)

(4) lit. For you will have a headache, beloved soul, if intoxication brings you to hangover.

(7-8) Layla and Majnun: the archetypal lovers of the Persian tradition, the latter named for his mad passion for Layla (*majnūn*: lit. insane).

Sleepless

(صبح دولت می‌دمد کو جام همچون آفتاب :14 ,*Diwān*)

(1) sun…fire: lit. کو جام همچون آفتاب (where is the cup like the sun?).

(7) Beautician: lit. مشاطه (comber, bride-dresser).

(8) lit. In the heart of the rose-leaf, sweetly conceals rose-water.

(10) Friend: lit. ساقی (*Sāqī*).

Fever

(آن شب قدری که گویند اهل خلوت امشب است :30 ,*Diwān*)

The Tangled Braid

(1) Night of Power (شب قدری): the first night of Qur'ānic revelation, celebrated during the last ten nights of Ramadān (c.f. the Qur'ān's eponymous 97th chapter); holy ones: lit. اهل خلوت (folk of the secluded chamber).

(4) remembering: i.e. practicing ذکر through chanting یا رب یا رب (O Lord! O Lord!).

(14) secret...kiss: lit. خنده زیر لب (laugh beneath the lip).

Return
(یا رب آن آهوی مشکین به ختن بازرسان :378 ,*Diwān*)

(1) Khutan: Khotan, in present-day China; known for its perfumes.

(3) our...flutist: lit. دل آزرده ما (our afflicted heart).

(10) Holy Dove: lit. عنقا (*'anqā*), a mythical bird invoked as a divine or prophetic symbol.

Shot from the Bow
(در دیر مغان آمد یارم قدحی در دست :23 ,*Diwān*)

(1) temple: lit. دیر مغان (temple of the Magians).

(8) glad...lovers: lit. افغان ز نظربازان برخاست (cries arose from the gaze-players).

Reading by the Light of Your Face
(دوش از مسجد سوی میخانه آمد پیر ما :10 ,*Diwān*)

(2) pious friends: lit. یاران طریقت (friends of the mystic path).

(3-4) Day of Alast: lit. عهد ازل (pre-eternal covenant); wise: lit. مغان (Magians).

(5) the shrine: lit. کعبه (*Ka'ba*), the sacred house of pilgrimage in Mecca.

(18) lit. Mercy upon your soul: beware of our arrow!

The World of Care
(بیا که قصر امل سخت سست بنیادست :37 ,*Diwān*)

(7) Lote-tree: i.e. سدره, a reference to the celestial lote-tree of the Qur'ān 53:14.

(20) world...sorrow: lit. جای فریادست (it is a place of lament).

(22) tranquil heart: lit. قبول خاطر (acceptance of heart).

The Falcon
(یاد باد آنکه سر کوی توام منزل بود :203 ,*Diwān*)

(6) loosening...knots: lit. بر شرح آنچه بر او مشکل بود (expounding that which was difficult for it).

(8) my strength: lit. سعی من و دل (my exertion [and that of the] heart).

(10) lit. I saw the wine jar; blood was in the heart, and head in the clay.

(12) reason: lit. مفتی عقل (the *muftī* of reason).

(13) the King: lit. بو اسحاقی (*Abū Ishāqī*), Persian Shah.

Love's Arsenal
(خم زلف تو دام کفر و دین است) (*Diwān*, 56:)

(3-4) shock: lit. معجز (miracle); mere rumor: lit. حدیث (saying, tradition); complete enchantment: lit. سحر مبین (patent sorcery), a Qur'ānic usage (see, for example, 46:7).

(9-10) is a wisdom: lit. is a scientific wonder (عجب علميست); core... universe: lit. چرخ هشتمش هفتم زمین است (its eighth sphere is the seventh land).

(12) those who record each word: lit. كرام الكاتبين (the noble writers), a quotation from the Qur'ān 82:11 and allusion to the two angels who record each person's deeds.

No Word
(دیرست که دلدار پیامی نفرستاد) (*Diwān*, 105:)

(5-8) lit. To me (of untamed character and agitated reason) / he sent neither deer-strider nor partridge-strutter. / He knew that the bird of my heart was to leave the hand / and he sent not a snare from his cheek-down, like a chain.

(9) friend: lit. ساقی (*Sāqī*).

(11) intimate union: lit. كرامات و مقامات (mystic miracles and stations).

This and That
(دردم از یار است و درمان نیز هم) (*Diwān*, 355:)

(15-16) The Police Force of True Religion: lit. محتسب (*muhtasib*, enforcer of Islamic orthodoxy); right hand man: lit. آصف (*Asif*); king: lit. سلیمان (*Sulaimān*).

Seduced
(دل از من برد و روی از من نهان کرد) (*Diwān*, 132:)

(3) seduced: lit. قصد جان (seeking [a] life; i.e. intending to kill); a phrase repeated also within lines 8 and 12.

(14) Love: lit. یار (friend).

(15) enemy: lit. عدو (antagonist), Qur'ānic term frequently applied to the Devil.

The Tangled Braid

Strangers
(روی تو کس ندید و هزارت رقیب هست :Diwān, 64)
  (2) lit. Yet in bud, there are a hundred nightingales [for] you.
  (12) lit. ناموس دیر راهب و نام صلیب (law of the monk's house, and the
  name of the cross).

The Road to Iraq
(یاد باد آن که ز ما وقت سفر یاد نکرد :Diwān, 138)
  (5) I soak...water: lit. کاغذین جامه به خوناب بشویم (I wash the papery robe
  in blood-water).
  (8) Farhad (فرهاد); the legendary lover of *Shīrīn* exiled to a mountain.
  (10) branches...hair: lit. شکن طره شمشاد (curl of the box-tree braid).
  (13) bride's beautician: lit. کلک مشاطه (the pen of the bride-dresser).
  (15) road to Iraq: a textual variant within the critical edition, alternate
  for the primary reading of road [to] Hijāz (راه حجاز).
  (17) Iraqi: i.e. the 13th-century Persian poet (عراقی).

Morning Prayer
(منم که گوشه میخانه خانقاه من است :Diwān, 54)
  (2) the secret words of the Sage: lit. دعای پیر مغان (the prayer of the
  Magian master).
  (8) hope: lit. خیال (vision, thought).
  (14) play along: lit. در طریق ادب کوش (strive in the path of good man-
  ners).

Words on the Heart
(در خرابات مغان نور خدا می‌بینم :Diwān, 349)
  (1) taverns of the wise: lit. خرابات مغان (Magian taverns).
  (5) idol's: lit. بتان (idols, objects of veneration).

Gone
(شربتی از لب لعلش نچشیدیم و برفت :Diwān, 85)
  (2) you were gone: lit. برفت (he/she departed).
  (5-6) prayer...the clock; Hafiz here mentions three particular prayers:
  Fātihah (the 1st chapter of the Qur'ān); *Harz-e Yamānī*; and *Ikhlās*
  (the 112th chapter of the Qur'ān).
  (10) he...us: lit. در گلستان وصالش نچمیدیم (we had not strolled in his rose-
  garden of union).

Insurrection
(به ملازمان سلطان که رساند این دعا را :Diwān, 6)

(3-4) Persian adaptation of the Muslim doxology (I take refuge in God from Satan, the accursed); brilliant, i.e. ثاقب (piercing; see the Qur'ān 86:3).

(11) insurrection: lit. قيامت (uprising, tumult, resurrection).

(13) Hafiz: lit. حافظ سحر خيز (Hafiz, the morning-riser).

On the Path
(اگر شراب خوری جرعهای فشان بر خاك :293 *Diwān*)

(6) the final Day: lit. روز واقعه (the Day of Happening), a reference to Judgment Day as characterized by the Qur'ānic chapter of the same name (i.e. *al-Wāqiʻa*, chapter 56).

(10) cosmic labyrinth: lit. دام مغاك (ensnaring abyss).

(14) poor ones: lit. اهل دل (the folk of the heart).

Niche
(بيا كه ترك فلك خوان روزه غارت كرد :127 *Diwān*)

(1-2) Bold...light: lit. ترك فلك (Turk of the sky); slim...moon, i.e. the lunar signal marking the conclusion of Ramadān (عيد, *ʻīd*).

(4) pilgrimage...fast (حج, روزه); two of the religious obligations of Islam.

(11) for...down: lit. نرگس جماش شيخ شهر (the raucous eye of the city's *shaykh*).

The Lantern
(ساقی بيا كه يار ز رخ پرده برگرفت :86 *Diwān*)

(5) fear of the Lord: i.e. تقوی (*taqvā*).

(10) one with the breath of Jesus: lit. عيسی دمی خدا بفرستاد (God sent a Jesus-breathed one).

(11) virgins, i.e. حوروش (*hūr*-like; see Overnight Delivery above).

Morning Wine
(كنون كه در چمن آمد گل از عدم به وجود :198 *Diwān*)

(10) lit. be free of the tradition of *ʻĀd* and *Thamūd* (i.e. عاد و ثمود); Qur'ānic reference to pre-Islamic peoples who rejected prophetic guidance (see the Qur'ān 7:73-74).

(16) lit. Now that the tulip has kindled Nimrod's fire; according to some Jewish and Muslim traditions, Abraham and Nimrod were contemporaries and religious adversaries.

(18) Column of Religion: partial translation of the name here memorialized, i.e. عماد دين محمود

113

The Tangled Braid

Learning by Heart

(واعظان كاين جلوه در محراب و منبر مى‌كنند :194 *Diwān*)

(6) judge: lit. در كار داور مى‌كنند ([shamefully] they act in the work of the [divine] Judge).

(8) wandering monks: lit. درويشان (dervishes).

(19) in the original, this line concludes with عقل گفت (Reason said:).

The Seed of Courage

(شنيده‌ام سخنى خوش كه پير كنعان گفت :88 *Diwān*)

(1-2) Jacob: lit. پير كنعان (old man of Canaan); an allusion to Jacob's painful separation from his beloved son Joseph (see the 12th chapter of the Qur'ān).

(3) sermon: lit. گفت واعظ شهر (spoken by the city preacher).

(9) lit. Me and the station of good-pleasure after this, and thanks [to the] guardian.

(16) courage: lit. خوشدلى (cheerfulness, sweet-heartedness).

Torn and Stained

(آنان كه خاك را به نظر كيميا كنند :191 *Diwān*)

(13-14) coat-of-many-colors: lit. پيراهنى (vest, shirt); the envious: lit. برادران غيور (envious brothers; see the Qur'ān 12:17-18).

(18) master: lit. صاحبدلان (companions of the heart).

Highway Robbery

(نيست در شهر نگارى كه دل ما ببرد :124 *Diwān*)

(10) lit. The master of gaze (صاحب نظرى) may take the name of this scene (نام تماشا).

(12) one glance: lit. نرگس تركانه (Turkish narcissus, beautiful eyes).

(14) idolater...Moses: lit. سامرى...يد بيضا (*Sāmirī*...the White hand), see the Qur'ān 20:85-88.

Ambush

(آن سيه چرده كه شيرينى عالم با اوست :59 *Diwān*)

(12) Jesus, son of Mary: lit. عيسى مريم (Jesus of Mary).

(14) lit. زانكه بخشايش بس روح مكرم با اوست (for the forgiveness of many [a] noble spirit is with him).

Eclipse

(خيال روى تو در هر طريق همره ماست :29 *Diwān*)

(6) See the Qur'ān 12:10-19.

(10) lit. So-and-So is of the corner-sitters of the dust of our court.

(11-14) The order of these final two stanzas is a variant from the critical text, which has them reversed.

The Breath of Jesus
(چه لطف بود که ناگاه رشحه قلمت :89 ,*Diwān*)
    (16) cup...Sultan: lit. شراب خضر ز جام جم (the drink of *Khizr* from the cup of *Jām*); for the former, see the Qur'ān 18:65-82.

Shelter
(هر که را با خط سبزت سر سودا باشد :153 ,*Diwān*)
    (1) face of the Friend: lit. خط سبزت (your verdant cheek-down).
    (11) shadow: lit. ظل ممدود (extended shade), a quotation from the Qur'ān 56:30.

Beneath the Veil
(بخت از دهان دوست نشانم نمی‌دهد :223 ,*Diwān*)
    (4) lit. She takes this not [from] me; and she gives that not [to] me.

The Work of Love
(دلا بسوز که سوز تو کارها بکند :182 ,*Diwān*)
    (3-4) Friend: lit. یار پریچهره (fairy-faced friend); every separation: lit. صد جفا (hundred cruelties, injustices).
    (7) considerate: lit. مسیحا دم (Messiah-breathed).
    (12) prayer: lit. فاتحه (the 1st chapter of the Qur'ān).

The Daughter of the Grape
(دوستان دختر رز توبه ز مستوری کرد :135 ,*Diwān*)
    (1) thrown...veil: lit. توبه ز مستوری کرد (repented of modesty).
    (9) your breeze: lit. نسیمش (his breath, breeze).
    (13-14) Satan, the proudly envious: lit. حسود (the envious, c.f. the Qur'ān 113:5); founded...illusion: lit. در سر مغروری (in arrogant desire).

Living Water
(خوشتر ز عیش و صحبت و باغ و بهار چیست :66 ,*Diwān*)
    (7) garden of paradise: lit. garden of *Iram* (روضه ارم), ancient locale mentioned in the Qur'ān 89:7.
    (15) the clear spring: lit. کوثر (see Escape Route above).

Love's Order
(دانی که چنگ و عود چه تقریر می‌کنند :195 ,*Diwān*)
    (2) police...apostasy: lit. تکفیر می کنند (they accuse of infidelity).

(16) tailor-shop: lit. کارخانه (work-house).

(17) saint: lit. شیخ (*shaykh*); preacher: lit. مفتی (*muftī*).

Wasted
(زلفت هزار دل به یکی تاره مو ببست :32 *Diwān*)

(12) lit. بر اهل وجد و حال در های و هو ببست (shut the door of hue and cry upon the folk of ecstasy and mystic states).

(14) lit. احرام طوف کعبه دل بی وضو ببست (put on the sacred garb [for] circumambulating the *Ka'ba* of the heart without [performing] ablutions).

A Gamble
(راهی بزن که آهی بر ساز آن توان زد :150 *Diwān*)

(1) strike...heart: lit. آهی...توان زد ([with which] one can utter a sigh).

(7-8) public worship: lit. در خانقه (in the [Sufi] cloister); cup of wisdom... wise: lit. می مغانه...مغان (Magian wine...Magians).

(19) in the power of the word: lit. به حق قرآن (by the truth of the Qur'ān).

Foundations
(در نمازم خم ابروی تو با یاد آمد :169 *Diwān*)

(2) quiet...gone: lit. محراب به فریاد آمد (the *mihrāb* came to cry out).

(12) true and gracious: lit. خداداد (God-given).

(14) without regret: از بار غم آزاد (free from grief's burden).

A Share in the Cup
(کی شعر خوش انگیزد خاطر که حزین باشد :157 *Diwān*)

(2) lit. یك نکته ازین دفتر گفتیم و همین باشد (We spoke one subtlety from the book, and thus it is).

(8) lit. His image is forbidden, even if he himself is a Chinese form-smith (صورتگر چین).

(11) As...wine: lit. در کار گلاب و گل (In the matter of rose-water and rose).

(14) he...them: lit. تا روز پسین باشد (it shall be until the last day).

Horizon
(سالها دفتر ما در گرو صهبا بود :199 *Diwān*)

(11) Drunk with bliss: lit. از درد محبت (from the pain of love).

(15-16) master: lit. پیر گلرنگ من (my master, Gulrang); Sufis...robes: lit. ازرق پوشان (the ones of azure attire); legends...spread: lit. ار نه حکایتها بود (if not, there were legends).

(18) counterfeit: lit. همه عیب نهان (all the concealed defects).

The Counterfeiter
(کنون که بر کف گل جام باده صاف است :45 *Diwān*,)
    (4) commentators on comments: lit. کشف کشاف (unveiling the *Unveiler*, i.e. Zamakhshari's celebrated work of Qur'ānic exegesis).
    (6) peak to peak: lit. قاف تا قاف (*Qāf* to *Qāf*); legendary mountain within Persian literature.
    (11-12) lit. The tradition of the accusers and the fancy of the fellow-laborers / Equal the story of the gold-sewer and the carpet-weaver.
    (13) chunks of gold: lit. زر سرخ (red gold).

Servant of the Cup
(صوفی بیا که آینه صافیست جام را :7 *Diwān*,)
    (1) friend: lit. صوفی (Sufi).
    (5) dove: lit. عنقا (*'anqā*); see Return above.
    (8) garden...wholeness: lit. روضه دارالسلام (paradisal garden, abode of *salām*; i.e. Eden).

Jasmine
(گل در بر و می در کف و معشوق به کام است :47 *Diwān*,)
    (5) book: lit. مذهب (school of thought; tradition).
    (15-16) lit. Why do you speak of shame? For my name is from shame / Why do you ask about name? For my shame is from name.
    (22) time of fasting: lit. عید صیام (the festival [concluding the month] of fasting).

Overdose
(تا ز میخانه و می نام و نشان خواهد بود :201 *Diwān*,)
    (2) master's path: lit. ره پیر مغان (road of the Magian master).
    (3) lit. حلقه پیر مغان از ازلم در گوش است (From pre-eternity, the Magian master's ring has been in my ear).
    (9-10) beloved: lit. ترک (Turk); capturing...nations: lit. تا دگر خون که از دیده روان خواهد بود (so that another's blood will flow from the eye).

The Drug
(بنفشه دوش به گل گفت و خوش نشانی داد :109 *Diwān*,)
    (2) You-Know-Who: lit. فلانی (see The Courier above).

The Tangled Braid

Drunk or Sober
(من و انکار شراب این چه حکایت باشد: Diwān, 154)
- (1) What a stupid idea: lit. این چه حکایت باشد (what a story is this?).
- (8) face of true communion: lit. عین ولایت (eye of companionship, essence of sainthood).
- (10) my baggage: lit. مستوری ما (our temperance).

The Clay Chalice
(دوش دیدم که ملایك در میخانه زدند: Diwān, 179)
- (2) our mortal clay: lit. گل آدم (the clay of Adam).
- (5) See the Qur'ān 33:72: We offered the trust [of faith] to the heavens and the earth and the mountains, but they refused to bear it, and were afraid of it; but humanity bore it....

Sugar
(تنت به ناز طبیبان نیازمند مباد: Diwān, 102)
- (4) May...path: lit. به هیچ عارضه شخص تو دردمند مباد (May your person never suffer affliction).
- (7) The earth...rug: در ان بساط که حسن تو (Upon that tract, wherein your beauty...).
- (10) flesh, spirit: lit. باطن ,ظاهر (exterior, interior); a customary Islamic dichotomy.
- (14) second-rate candy: lit. علاج گلاب و قند (remedy of rose-water and sugar).

Transformations
(ستارهای بدرخشید و ماه مجلس شد: Diwān, 163)
- (15-16) The critical text has an additional stanza here (خیال آب خضر...) which we have omitted.
- (18) transformation: lit. کیمیای (i.e. kīmiyā; cognate of English chemistry, alchemy).

Headless
(کسی که حسن خط دوست در نظر دارد: Diwān, 112)
- (1) unseen...friend: lit. حسن خط دوست (beauty of the friend's cheek-down).
- (6) your lover: lit. کسی به وصل تو...یافت پروانه (The one who obtained license for union with you).
- (12) the seductive whisperings: i.e. وسوسه, satanic temptations (see the Qur'ān 114:4-5).

The Mirror of Princes

(دلم جز مهر مهرویان طریقی بر نمی‌گیرد :145 ,*Diwān*)

   (3) about the beloved: lit. از خط ساقی (about the cheek-down of the *Sāqī*).

   (15) mirror of princes: lit. آن آئینه (that mirror; see Loss in Translation above).

At the Foot of the Wine-cask

(اگر چه عرض هنر پیش یار بی‌ادبیست :65 ,*Diwān*)

   (8) prophet, the enemy: lit. مصطفوی, بولهب; the prophet Muhammad and his antagonist Abū Lahab (see the Qur'ān 111:1).

   (12) veil of the purple in the glass: lit. نقاب زجاجی و پرده عنبیست (veil of glass and curtain of grape).

   (15) worn…begging: lit. مدامم استظهار (Constantly mine [is the] seeking of assistance).

A Game of Glances

(عکس روی تو چو بر آینه جام افتاد :107 ,*Diwān*)

   (10) Day of Alast: lit. عهد ازل (pre-eternal covenant).

Hooked

(یارم چو قدح به دست گیرد :144 ,*Diwān*)

   (8) policeman: lit. محتسبی (see This and That above).

On the Shore

(حاصل کارگه کون و مکان این همه نیست :75 ,*Diwān*)

   (5) sidra…Tree of Paradise, i.e. سدره و طوبی; for the former, see the Qur'ān 53:14.

Thrown

(دیده دریا کنم و صبر به صحرا فکنم :340 ,*Diwān*)

   (4) sin of Eve and Adam: i.e. yielding to temptation, and exile from paradise (Qur'ān 7:22).

   (5-6) by the Light: lit. فلك ([of] the sky); neck of its quiver: lit. ترکش جوزا (the quiver of Gemini).

The Flood

(بلبلی خون جگر خورد و گلی حاصل کرد :130 ,*Diwān*)

   (1) source of envy: lit. خون جگر (blood of the liver).

   (4) flash-flood of nothingness: lit. سیل فنا (flood of annihilation).

   (5) refresh my thirsty gaze: lit. قرة العین (the cooling of the eye), a

The Tangled Braid

Qur'ānic phrase signifying consolation or delight (see, for example, the Qur'ān 19:26).
(10) these elements: lit. كهگل (plaster of mud and straw).

Shipwrecked
(دل می‌رود ز دستم صاحبدلان خدا را :5 *Diwān*)
(5) At...seems: lit. ده روزه مهر گردون (For ten days, the affection of the globe).
(17) squeamish: lit. زاهد (ascetic).
(20) drink: lit. کیمیای (chemistry, elixir); Qarun: see The Orchard of Delight above.

The Arc
(دست در حلقه آن زلف دوتا نتوان کرد :133 *Diwān*)
(6) orthodox mock you: lit. به فسوسی که کند خصم (for the reproach which the antagonist makes).
(9) the hymns: lit. سماع (recital, spiritual concert).
(18) whole creation: lit. خلق خدا (God's creatures).
(20) for us: lit. در مذهب ما (in our school, tradition).

The Pearl
(خلوت گزیده را به تماشا چه حاجت است :34 *Diwān*)
(1) monk in his cell: lit. خلوت گزیده (the one who has chosen the *khalvat*); see The Courier above.